DO·IT·YOURSELF

OUTDOOR
PROJECTS

Sterling Publishing Co., Inc.   New York

Published by
Sterling Publishing Co, Inc.
387 Park Avenue South, New York,
NY 10016-8810

© Marshall Cavendish Limited 1988

Second impression 1989

ISBN 0-8069-6948-2

BOMC offers recordings and compact discs, cassettes
and records. For information and catalog write to
BOMR, Camp Hill, PA 17012.

Typeset by J&L Composition, Filey,
North Yorkshire, England

Printed and bound in Hong Kong

This material was previously published in the
Marshall Cavendish partwork *Do It Right*.

Picture Credits

John Badminton: 36–39.
Halls Homes & Gardens: 90–94
Dave King: 18–23, 25, 26, 28, 30, 31, 76, 78–80.
Steve Lyne: 14–17, 32–35, 54–61, 81–84, 95, 97–99, 109.
Alan Marsh: 10–13, 40–44, 46–53, 62, 64, 65, 71, 74, 75, 80(b), 85, 87–89.
Robin Scagell: 100.
Therm-a-Stor Ltd: 45.
Gareth Trevor: 66, 68–70, 101–103.

▲ CONTENTS

▲ INTRODUCTION

An obvious advantage of constructing your own projects is that you can adapt designs to suit your exact requirements, and usually save money at the same time. It is also a pleasurable pastime. The projects in this book have been carefully designed, and some alternative design ideas are included to help you on your way. There are, broadly speaking, two categories: those entitled Projects which are all constructed from basic materials; and those entitled Weekenders which include constructions from kits and some maintenance tasks (as the name implies, you should be able to complete these in a weekend).

The projects here are for all areas of your yard. There are planters, a greenhouse and a sunspace for the avid gardener, and a reclining sunbed for those who prefer to be simply loungers. If you don't mind digging, how about building a garden pond, complete with fountain and waterfall to complement it? And when the sundial indicates a mealtime, lay down your Do-it-Yourself tools and relax on the picnic bench to a barbecue on the patio.

Each project is accompanied by a Checklist of the tools and materials that you will need to complete it so you should not find that, part of the way through the job, you are missing some vital item. A list of optional items is also included.

Much of the satisfaction of doing-it-yourself is measured by the quality of the end result. Cross-references are given in each project to the relevant pages in the Skills Guide at the end of the book so, if you are uncertain about

any of the techniques involved, you can refer to them. Read through the instructions for the project from start to finish before commencing work so that you have an overall picture of what is involved.

When buying materials for concreting and masonry jobs, allow an extra five percent above the amount you have estimated — it is infuriating to run out just when the end is in sight! With woodworking projects, remember that standard lumber sizes are nominal, so it is important to check the actual dimensions of the wood you are using before working out critical dimensions. Always remember when marking out to check and double check all dimensions before proceeding — a pencil line on a piece of wood is easy to erase and reposition, but if it is cut undersize, it can be costly to replace and will cause frustration. A good carpenter will only use a cutting list as a guide — at each stage of the construction, the dimensions of the parts being cut to size should be measured to fit exactly.

Finally, a few notes on safety. Do read manufacturers' instructions carefully before using equipment with which you are not familiar. Avoid wearing loose clothing when using power tools as it can become entangled and cause serious injury, and keep the cord over your shoulder out of the way. Always unplug power tools before making any adjustments. When carrying building materials, several light loads are better than a few strenuous ones. Finally, allow yourself plenty of time to complete the job to make sure that the end result is of the high quality that you deserve.

MIKE TRIER

Brick Planter

There are a few specialist tools you need for this project (such as trowels and a level) but you can save money by making some yourself. The simplest tool is a strike board which is nothing more than a straight piece of 2 × 4 or similar sized lumber.

A gauge rod or story pole is an invaluable tool which is used to check the thicknesses of the mortar courses. To make a gauge rod, mark off a strip of wood with brick and mortar thicknesses.

A third tool you can make yourself, a builder's square, is described in the Skills Guide p. 124.

Though the planter can be free-standing, the chances are that you will want to incorporate it into a patio design or even butt it up against the side of a wall. On this last point, one word of warning: if you build the planter against the side of your house, be sure to prime the wall with a couple of coats of a waterproofing compound before you start on the construction – this will prevent any problems which might be caused by the moisture in the soil coming in constant contact with the fabric of the wall.

A brick planter, filled with an assortment of shrubs and flowers, will give your yard a new lease on life. It's easy to adapt the planter's size and shape to suit your situation and the plants you have in mind.

Just about every yard, whether it is large or small, will benefit from a raised planter – 'terraced' levels of greenery create an effect that's interesting to the eye and easier on the back. This one is particularly easy to build because it employs a simple running bond and there is no need to chop any bricks in half.

The planter must be built on sturdy foundations sunk into the ground – 6in of concrete should be sufficient unless the soil in your area is very sandy. Obviously, if your garden is on a slope, you will have to excavate and level the foundation.

Four horizontal courses and a top row of vertical or 'soldier' bricks will bring the planter up to an ideal height for variegated plants – an extra course will probably make it too tall but if you plan to plant large shrubs or tall grasses, you may prefer to have just two or three horizontal courses.

Bricks come in many different colors and finishes. If you can, try to get hold of some second-hand ones as they will be comparatively inexpensive and will have an attractive 'weathered' look. If you have to buy new bricks for a project such as this where they will be exposed to the elements, use MW (medium weathering) facing bricks.

CHECKLIST

Tools
bricklayer's trowel
level
pointing trowel (optional)
tape measure

Homemade tools
builder's square
strike board
gauge rod
line and blocks (or pins)

Materials
bricks
cement and sand for mortar
cement, sand,
¾ in aggregate for concrete
waterproofer and mortar
colorant (optional)

See Skills Guide
pp. 123, 124, 125.

DESIGNS FOR A BRICK PLANTER

Although the depth of the planter, like all the other dimensions, is variable, it's both practical and convenient to keep the trench about 8in wide. This means that you won't have to cut any bricks in half and consequently the bricklaying (and estimating) is made that much easier.

A soldier course of bricks is only one way of finishing off the top of the planter. If you prefer, you can use special coping stones or lay bricks frog-down.

It is important to have a number of weep holes in the bottom course — without them, the soil will become waterlogged.

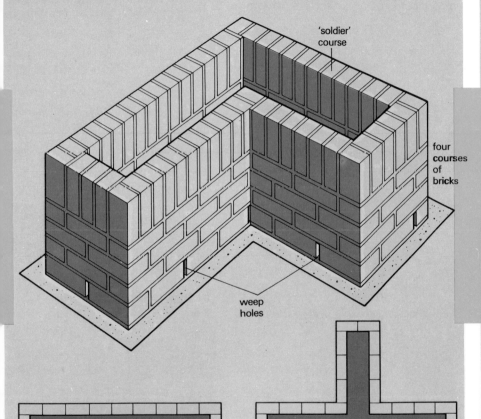

'soldier' course

four courses of bricks

weep holes

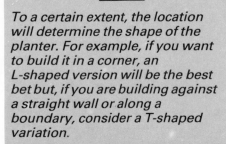

To a certain extent, the location will determine the shape of the planter. For example, if you want to build it in a corner, an L-shaped version will be the best bet but, if you are building against a straight wall or along a boundary, consider a T-shaped variation.

If you want to create a more interesting feature, why not build a planter in the shape of a cross? With a little forethought it's even possible to vary the heights.

Make a few sketches of how you visualize the planter before you start work — if this is done to scale, so much the better.

LAY THE FOUNDATIONS

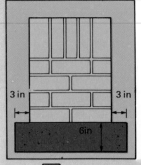

3 in   3 in

6in

The concrete should be 6in deep and must extend beyond the walls below ground level

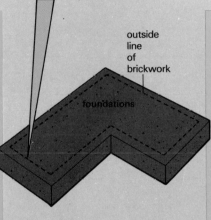

outside line of brickwork

foundations

Excavate a shallow trench for the foundations, bearing in mind that the concrete should extend 3in beyond the brickwork.

Mix up the cement, sand and aggregate in the ratio 1:3:6 and pour the concrete into the trench. Level off the concrete with your strike board and allow to set.

MARK OUT THE WALLS

Dry-lay the first course, check that the angles are square, then set up lines and score the concrete

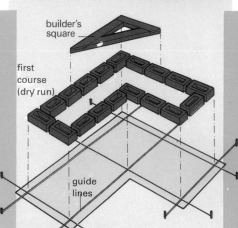

builder's square

first course (dry run)

guide lines

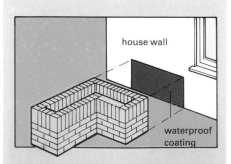

house wall

waterproof coating

If you want to build the planter against a house wall, you must take steps to prevent moisture from causing problems along the house wall. The easiest way to protect it is to paint it with at least two coats of a waterproofing compound. There are several such compounds currently available on the market.

LAY THE FIRST COURSE

When you lay the first course, leave every alternate vertical joint unmortared – these gaps will serve as weep holes and will ensure that the soil in the finished planter is adequately drained. Alternatively, complete a whole course then rake out the damp mortar.

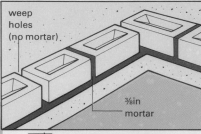

weep holes (no mortar)

⅜in mortar

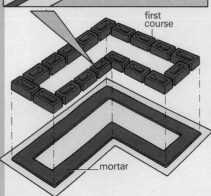

first course

mortar

Butter the end of each brick before laying it

Use a large trowel to spread a bed of mortar, about ⅜in thick, on top of the concrete. Then, beginning from a corner, start laying the first course. It is easier if you 'butter' the end of each brick with mortar before positioning it and tapping it into place level with the last one.

BUILD UP THE CORNERS

It is good bricklaying technique to build up the corners and then to lay the intermediate bricks. The bricks should overlap each other

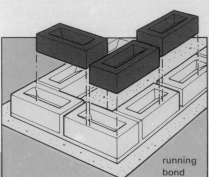

running bond

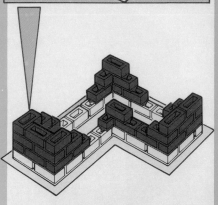

As you construct each corner, check that it is plumb at frequent intervals and use your gauge rod to judge the thicknesses of the mortar courses. There is a definite knack to laying bricks successfully and this only comes with practice. It helps if you work to a rhythm.

COMPLETE THE COURSES

To help you position the intermediate bricks accurately, rig up a guide line. Hold the line taut with wooden blocks (below) or with steel pins – tap each brick until it's level with the taut line

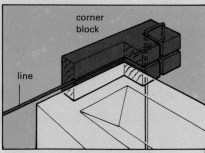

corner block

line

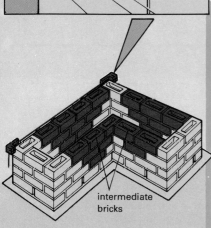

intermediate bricks

Check the level of the wall often

As you complete each course, check that it is level. If you only have a short level, you can effectively extend it by taping it on top of a long, straight piece of wood. If a brick stands proud, tap it back into place with the heel of your trowel. Exercise particular care at the corners.

ADD THE SOLDIER COURSE

The soldier course is a decorative feature of the wall so align each brick with care as you lay it on end, vertically

Tap the bricks into place with the heel of your trowel

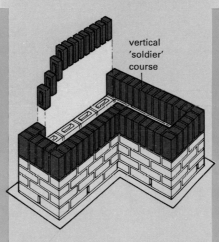

vertical 'soldier' course

Arrange the soldier course in a dry-run before you start mortaring the bricks in place – you may find that the gaps have to be less than ⅜in.

POINT THE WALLS

To get a round pointing profile, rub over the mortar joints with a piece of garden hose or a short length of dowel

Point the joints with a piece of hose

pointing

It's best to point each section of the planter as it is completed, otherwise the mortar may set hard. Clean up dirty bricks with a wire brush.

Three-in-one Picnic Bench

If you want to sit in the sunshine and occasionally picnic, if you want to train climbing plants and store small garden tools, if you want to make good use of space, then this wall-mounted bench is what you need

Most local garden centers don't stock a wide range of garden furniture and they rarely stock what you want. So if you want seating and a picnic table, if you want a climbing frame and planter to brighten up a featureless wall, and if you want to store assorted gardening tools for a bit of casual caretaking, you've got a problem. You'll either need to buy three (or more) different items or you'll need to make your own.

Here's a practical design that serves all three purposes and that can be easily adapted to fit the space available, the plants you want to train and the tools you need to store in the bench.

The three-in-one bench is wall-mounted – attached to a house or garden wall with sturdy masonry bolts – so that it's out of the way and in the best sun trap your garden has to offer. The wall fastenings make it secure as a bench and table and mean that you can cultivate climbing plants in the plant tray that's part of the design.

The slatted seat runs from one end to the other to form the top of the tool storage box. Exterior grade plywood and weather resistant red cedar in the sizes specified make it a durable, as well as a practical, garden feature.

CHECKLIST

Tools
try square, tape measure, handsaw, jigsaw or saber saw, backsaw, screwdrivers, utility knife, drill and assorted bits (including ¾in masonry bit and 1⅛in spade bit or hole saw), miter box (optional), wooden mallet, ¾in bevel edged chisel.

Materials
Softwood: 4 × 4
3 × 3, 1 × 2, 1 × 3, ½ × 1
plywood: ¼in
trellis and frame (optional)
(2in) butt hinges
latch, two 6in
masonry bolts,
building paper and
adhesive,
waterproof adhesive,
wood preservative

See Skills Guide pp. 112, 113, 117 and 122.

WORKING OUT THE DESIGN

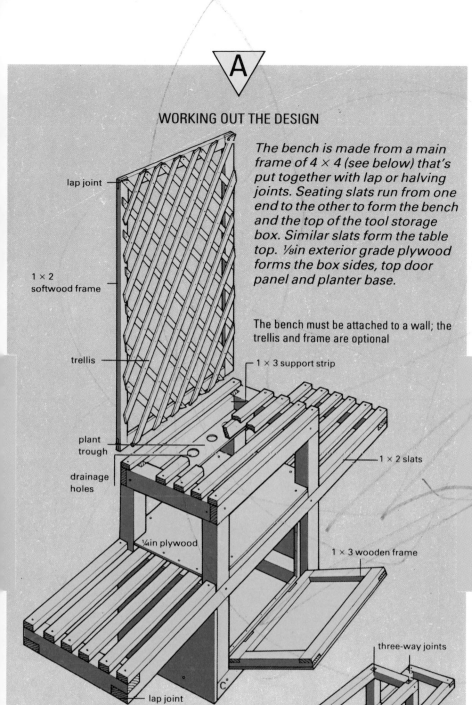

lap joint

1 × 2 softwood frame

trellis

plant trough

drainage holes

¼in plywood

1 × 3 support strip

1 × 2 slats

1 × 3 wooden frame

lap joint

three-way joints

three-way joint

the seat's carcase

The bench is made from a main frame of 4 × 4 (see below) that's put together with lap or halving joints. Seating slats run from one end to the other to form the bench and the top of the tool storage box. Similar slats form the table top. ⅛in exterior grade plywood forms the box sides, top door panel and planter base.

The bench must be attached to a wall; the trellis and frame are optional

You can adapt sizes to suit the spaces available, or you can build it using the dimensions given here, but you must work out alterations carefully beforehand. The bench shown is 30in high, 7ft long, with a table top 3ft wide and 18in deep. The seating level is 18in from the base, so the three-way through joints (see right) must be marked and cut accordingly. The easiest dimensions to alter are the length of seats and table top.

Make the main frame from 4 × 4 lumber, then add the slats followed by the plywood. Once you've cut the parts (see right), the main difficulty will be in cutting the three-way joints.

CUTTING THE FRAME PARTS

Use a try square and knife to mark all around

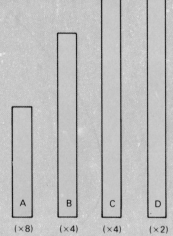

A	B	C	D
(×8)	(×4)	(×4)	(×2)

Cut out the frame lengths and check that they all match and that the ends are perfectly square

Choose a suitable length for the full bench (D), then calculate the length of the table section (C). Try not to alter the height and depth (B and A) – you'll find that 30in is an ideal height while a depth of 18in is both comfortable and practical. For the size shown you need eight parts A (18in) four parts B (30in) for the bench height, four parts C (36in) to a length of your choice for the table top and box, and two parts D (7ft or more).

2

ASSEMBLE THE FRAME

Begin with three way joints at the top of B. Mark C/B as a halving, then A/B as a halving, then trim the ends of parts A to fit against C and B

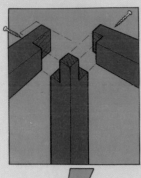

Label the parts you have cut. Mark seat height (for D) 18in from the base

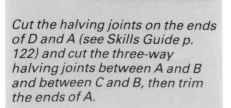

Three-way joints between A/B and D are much like the joints at the top, except that D is a 'through' component

2x   2x

2in No 8

Cut the halving joints on the ends of D and A (see Skills Guide p. 122) and cut the three-way halving joints between A and B and between C and B, then trim the ends of A.

3

ADD SEATING SLATS

Drill holes at either end of one part D before you attach the slats: you need these holes for the masonry bolts which secure the bench

The slats form the seating and act as a base for the plywood box top. Cut them to length, screw to parts A and D, then smooth off corners

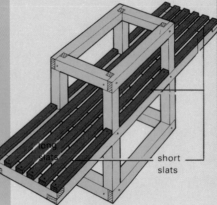

long slats

short slats

You need six slats in all, but with regular spaces between them

Assemble the frame with waterproof glue and screws, but leave the top parts A and C dry to remove them later. Attach 1 × 2 slats to span the length, cutting as necessary.

4

ADD PLYWOOD BOX CLADDING

Measure, cut and attach the plant trough base in the same way, but drill a series of 1in diameter holes in it to allow for drainage. Choose a depth of trough to suit the pots or trays for the plants you have in mind – when you come to attach the table slats, just leave a vacant space above the trough. Make the drain holes with a spade bit or hole saw (see panel right).

Allow the box top to overlap the box sides so that the exposed veneer of the side panels are given added weather protection.

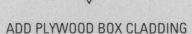

plant trough

drainage holes

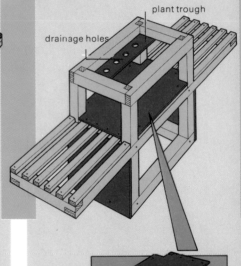

corner cutouts

Remove the top parts A and C to secure the box top. Attach the parts to secure the trough base

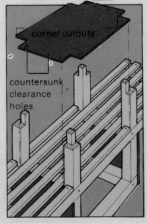

countersunk clearance holes

¼in exterior grade plywood forms the top and sides of the box and the base of the plant trough. Cut to fit and attach with ¾in screws. Allow the top to overlap the sides to protect them.

ADD TABLE SLATS AND DOOR

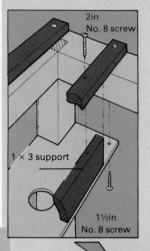

2in No. 8 screw

1 × 3 support

1½in No. 8 screw

You'll need to support the inside edge of the trough with a length of 1 × 4 board. Screw it to the nearest slat

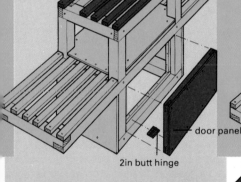

door panel

2in butt hinge

Measure the opening and cut the plywood to fit, then add the framing. Attach the slats with screws

Assemble the door and make a door stop of small beading. Hinge the door at the bottom using alloy or plastic butt hinges

Attach the slats for the table top in the same way as the seats, but with special provision for the trough (above). Make a door from halving-jointed framing faced with ¼in plywood.

ATTACH TO A WALL

building paper

6in masonry bolt

Place the bench against the wall to mark for masonry bolts. The loose-head type will be easier

It's best to construct a rough base for the bench: use concrete or loose paving slabs

foundations

Apply a layer of waterproofing paint to the side that goes against the wall, then add a layer of building paper as a vapor barrier

Use masonry bolts to attach the bench to a brick house or garden wall. Construct a rough base too – it's not vital but it's a good idea to cast a concrete slab or lay pavers.

FINISHING OFF

Put plant pots or trays into the trough and erect a trellis frame to train climbing plants up the wall above. Add a latch or lock. Finish with varnish or preservative.

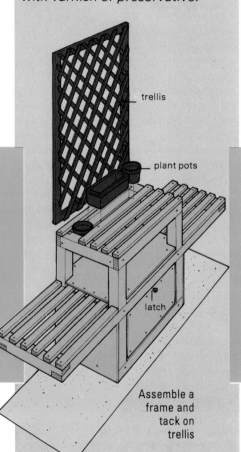

trellis

plant pots

latch

Assemble a frame and tack on trellis

★ Drill attachments

You'll find a hole saw useful for making the holes in the trough. A screwdriver attachment will make light work of all the screwing.

Erect a Shed

Even the most modest gardener can amass a considerable armory of tools and equipment and the ideal place to store them – along with any other household paraphernalia – is in a humble tool shed. There's a diverse range of styles and sizes to suit all gardens – and assembly is quick and uncomplicated.

Storing garden tools can be a real bugbear. Bicycles, deckchairs and so on can also clutter the home – and you should never keep large quantities of chemicals and paint indoors, for obvious safety reasons.

One answer is to buy a garden shed. You don't need an extensive yard in order to locate it. Compact models are available which can fit snugly into a small corner and won't commandeer valuable fertile soil.

On the other hand investing in a larger model with ample headroom and windows will not only provide storage space but can double as a potting shed or workshop.

Traditional garden buildings are wooden, but there are also tough metal storage sheds on the market. These last longer in the face of adverse climatic conditions, but can look utilitarian and are sometimes more costly.

1 What the job involves

Whatever the style of shed you choose, most are available in self-assembly form, comprising pre-fabricated wall panels, roof and floor. Assembly is typically a matter of bolting, screwing or nailing the sections together.
● Take time to choose a shed that will suit your needs (see Options).
● Prepare the site foundations, making sure that it is level and has adequate drainage. See Skills Guide pp. 130–133.
● Lay paving slabs – or cast a concrete pad on which you can erect the shed.
● Assemble the shed floor on its wooden supports set on vapor barrier to help keep it dry.
● Erect the shed walls.
● Add the roof panels.
● Weatherproof the roof.
● Add the door and window if necessary, then glaze the panes.

CHECKLIST

Tools
wrench
hammer
screwdriver
shovel
wheelbarrow
electric drill
level

Materials
paving slabs or concrete (for foundations)
kit of parts for shed
   (including all hardware)
rolls of roofing felt
1in large-headed
   galvanized roofing nails
glaziers points if necessary

See Skills Guide pp. 116, 130, 131, 132, 133

Attach door and window hardware, and finish off the project by putting up shelves and hooks etc.

Ensure the shed kit contains all you need including hardware, screws, and other fastenings

BEFORE YOU START

- choose the shed that best suits your needs (See Options). Visit a garden center or do it yourself store to see what best suits your needs.
- decide on the shed's location: a level, freely-draining site is necessary. Don't place it at the far end of the yard unless there's a path to it – it may be better close to the house, especially for a power supply.
- Make sure it has heavy duty locks to deter burglars from breaking in.
- collect together all the tools and materials you'll need to assemble and finish the shed (or check that they're included in the kit), as well as preservative if the wooden panels haven't been pre-treated to make sure it will last and withstand the elements.

! WATCH OUT FOR

- uneven ground. Level the earth and make sure it is free-draining.
- lumber that hasn't been treated; you'll need to buy preservative to protect the shed.
- flimsy hardware, like latches; you can always change them.
- flimsy construction. Test the rigidity of a display shed by slamming the door and shaking the walls.

Options

Size of shed is your first decision when choosing. A popular size is about 6ft 6in deep × 5ft wide, allowing ample storage space plus room for a shelf and folding workbench. If the shed is just for storage, one with an area of about 3ft sq should be adequate — though you won't be able to step inside. A large shed with window and a light can double as a workshop.

There are two main roof profiles for garden sheds: the 'apex' has a pitch, or slope, at each side of the ridge; the shed has a slope in only one direction. Apex roofs give good overall headroom and are best if you're tall and want to work inside the shed. Shed roofs usually have the high side on the window wall, anticipating a bench below; the lower side is for storage.

The type of wood used, and how it is treated, plays an important role in a shed's durability. Most softwoods need treating regularly with preservative to stave off rot. Some sheds are sold untreated but it's best to choose one that's been pressure-impregnated with preservative. Western Red Cedar is the exception as it is a naturally durable timber which weathers to a subtle grey (treat it with a brush-on liquid to restore the light brown tone).

Cladding used to form the wall panels of the shed can be either tapered wood siding (where horizontal boards overlap those below); rabbeted shiplap (with a distinctive curved rabbet between interlocking horizontal boards); or V-jointed tongue and groove boarding, used vertically (for a flat finish with a neat V-shaped groove between boards).

A floor is an important option unless the shed is to be erected on a concrete base. It may consist of wood framing covered with exterior-grade plywood or conventional floorboards. The shed can be set directly onto a concrete base without its own floor.

Doors and windows can be specified in various positions, depending on the style of shed. Shed roof structures usually have the window (which may be fixed or an awning type) on the front and the door on the front or at one end. You can usually choose between having the door on the left or right of the window. Apex roof sheds usually have a door at one end and windows on both sides.

A building paper internal lining to prevent drafts and moisture penetration is an option which will increase the shed's durability.

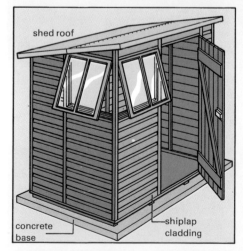

Shed roof sheds normally have the windows and door at the side where there is most headroom

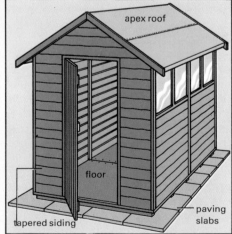

Apex roof sheds tend to have the door set into one gable end and windows in one or both sides

2 Laying the foundations

1. Give the shed a firm foundation by laying paving slabs on a bed of gravel covered with sand

2. Having gently tapped the slabs in place with the handle of a hammer, check that they are level

Although you can lay a shed with a wooden floor directly on firm sub-soil, it would soon succumb to the effect of dampness – namely rot. It's far better to prepare a solid base, and this is easiest to make using concrete paving slabs. Alternatively, you can construct a solid concrete base over 3in of gravel. (See Skills Guide pp. 130, 131, 133.)

Slabs are sold in various sizes – commonly about 18in square – and in a range of colors, typically reds, browns, buff tones and yellows. Choose which you prefer, remembering that the larger the slab, the less likelihood there is of uneven settlement. Buy sufficient slabs to cover the base of the shed with an overlap of about 4in all around.

Mark out the area of the slab base on the ground, using stringlines and pegs. Remove any vegetation and large stones and transfer the fertile topsoil to another part of the yard. If the area is grassed, lift the turfs, roll them up and store them for possible re-use elsewhere.

Use a garden roller to compact and flatten the earth, or tamp it down with a heavy wooden post (wear gloves to protect your hands from splinters) or a sledgehammer. Apply a liberal dose of weedkiller to the ground to prevent weeds growing up between the slabs.

There are other options you could use for larger outbuildings – like concrete posts laid on top of brick piers – but average sheds won't require them.

★ TIP

If the ground is soft in patches, fill in hollows with a little fine aggregate and ram this down with a sledgehammer to firm up the base. Add sand on top to provide a cushion for the slabs and so prevent them from breaking as you lay them over the aggregate.

Spread an even, 2in layer of sand over the sub-base then lay the slabs on top, tapping them down gently with the handle of a club hammer. Allow the base to be a number of whole slabs across.

Place a level on a long straight-edged plank and span the area of slabs; if any of the slabs are uneven, remove excess sand or fill in with more, as necessary.

★ TIP

Lay a few extra slabs in front of the doorway – or better still, run a pathway right up to the slab base – to prevent the grass being worn away and the bare earth being dug into a mudbath.

3 Assembling the floor

Treat the floor components with preservative, if necessary, then attach the floor panels or boards to the wooden supports. With some shed kits, the floor may be pre-assembled, although you may need to piece together sections.

With a boarded floor, nail the boards to the tops of the supports which should be spaced evenly apart – use a measured length of wood to assure this. With a panel floor, the panels may have slim supports, which rest on top of heavier posts. Join panels together by toe nailing through one panel into the slim supports of the abutting panel. Nail the wooden strips together, too.

Place strips of building paper on the slab base underneath each wooden support to protect the wood against moisture. Make sure the vapor barrier is wider than the supports. You can lay a sheet of roofing felt under the entire shed floor, or simply cut out strips approximately 9in wide, and lay each strip separately.

Place a level on the floor assembly to check that it's level. If it's badly out of true you'd be wise to adjust the slab base; if it's only a little uneven, pack under the supports with wooden shims.

Before laying the floor, protect the bearers from moisture with strips of roofing felt

4 Erecting the walls

1. Temporarily join the wall panels together, starting with an end panel and one side

2. Ensure the walls are square before joining them permanently and nailing them to the floor

You'll need assistance in assembling the wall panels, unless you use temporary braces. Start assembling the panels at a corner. Lift up the panels – a side and back panel are easiest to erect first.

Align the framing members of the panels inside and outside and ensure that they're even along the top edge. With bolt-together sections, slot the connecting bolts through the pre-drilled holes from the outside and screw on the nuts inside finger-tight. There are usually three connection points per corner – one at top and bottom; one in the center.

★ TIP

With some sheds you have to nail the panels together. Drive in the nails at opposite angles to each other to prevent them pulling out; don't drive them in fully so you can make adjustments later. Other shed panels are screwed together: again, temporarily nail them.

Position the corner assembly accurately on the shed floor. Consult the maker's instructions here – the panels are usually meant to overhang the floor by 1in or so. Large shed walls may comprise two or more panels: lift these up one by one and secure to the positioned corner panels.

Lift up the remaining panels and

3. Nail trimming strips into the gap between the side walls at each of the corners

attach to the assembly. Make sure you fit panels the right way up: if it's not obvious, the top cross piece is usually thicker than the cross piece at the bottom.

Put in the window panels in the same way.

With all four sides erected, measure the internal diagonals to check that the walls are square – the dimensions should be equal. Make adjustments then either tighten the bolts using a wrench or drill pilot holes for the screws and drive them home, or drive any nails fully in. Nail the base strips of the wall panels to the floor.

5 Adding a roof

1. Nail roof panels to the apex walls and reinforce the ridge with plates nailed to rafters inside

With the shed walls erected you can add the roof panels. The roof construction varies with the type of shed: with some types the boards are secured with metal brackets to the wall frames, with others they're simply nailed from below or above.

A shed roof should slope away from the door and window side – the slope is formed by screwing a header beam at the front and tapered splays down each side. Lift these one at a time on top of the wall panels, and use a bradawl to start off the screw holes before screwing them into place.

A central roof support is usually added between the front and back walls: position it and nail into its ends through the header and rear top cross piece. Position the roof board or boards so they overhang the edges evenly all round. Secure the boards by screwing into them through the top roof supports or by nailing from above into the top members of the shed at 6in intervals.

Apex roofs can be harder to put up. On small sheds the boards are usually simply nailed to the wall frames and the ridge reinforced at each end with a plywood plate. Larger sheds may include rafters – sometimes even trusses – to support the roof's weight.

Unless the roof boards are pre-felted, lay roofing felt on top. Use a

6 Doles...

2. Add roofing felt with ridge and edge overlaps. Secure it in place with large headed roofing nails

36in wide felt, usually supplied with the shed.

Unroll the felt and leave it for 48 hours – preferably in a warm room – so that it will stretch and flatten, reducing the risk of wrinkling. Work on a warm day so the felt is pliable.

With a shed roof structure, start at the lower edge of the roof and lay a strip of felt horizontally. Lay second – and subsequent – strips overlapping the one below generously by at least 4in. Secure the felt to the roof boards with ¾ galvanized large-headed roofing nails driven through both layers of felt at 4in intervals. Some shed kits include waterproof adhesive to seal the joints. On smaller sheds the roofing felt is sometimes secured with thin laths nailed on top.

Trim the felt so that it overhangs the roof by about 2in and nail it to the edges of the roof boards. Nail the fascia boards to the front and sides of the roof boards.

Felt an apex roof by laying strips of felt on the lower edges of each pitch then add a single piece over the ridge and strips for best effect. Nail at the joins as described above and fit angled bargeboards to the gabled ends of the roof.

6 Doors

Glazing can simply be pinned in place without putty. Doors are often pre-fitted in a wall panel

The door (and any opening window) is usually hung on black finished tee hinges. If pilot screw holes are not pre-drilled, get your helper to hold the door in position with a ¼in clearance at the bottom, while you mark the hinge hole positions against it and the frame.

Drill pilot holes then screw the hinges first to the door, then lift it up and screw to the frame. Do likewise with an opening window.

For minimum security, add a hasp and staple to the door so that you can protect the shed contents with a padlock. Larger sheds may include key-operated rim locks.

⭐ **TIP**

For extra security, you can bolt the hinges, as well as the hasp and staple, to the door and frame. This will prevent anyone from simply unscrewing the door to break in.

Windows will probably need glazing and putty and glass may be supplied with the kit. Roll the putty into sausages and line the rabbet, then press the pane into place. Secure the glass on the outside with glazier's points or small brads before applying more putty, bevelled to shed water. Alternatively, retain the glass with a wooden strip, sandwiching putty between it and the glass.

7 Finishing off

Complete the shed with trimming strips. Where wall panels meet at the corners, there'll be a recess into which you nail 1 × 1 strips to seal the join.

Inside the shed, line the walls to stop drafts with tempered hardboard cut to fit between the center of one frame panel and the next. Secure with 1in brads every 6in. You can also sandwich insulation between the hardboard and walls. Alternatively, use sheets of building paper stapled to the framework.

You may be offered shelves to add to your shed: these are usually simple boards on a stiffening frame, and rest on brackets screwed to the wall panels.

1. Neaten the gable ends of the roof by nailing the angled bargeboards and finials in place

2. Finish off the interior with shelves and tool hooks ensuring the support brackets are secure

A Garden Pond

A pond is an attractive feature in any flower garden and, once stocked, needs little attention to keep it lively and interesting. Digging the hole may be hard work but isn't complicated — it's perfectly possible to finish the pond in a single day.

Almost all types of flower garden will benefit from a pond. Once stocked with plants and fish, it adds color and interest and soon attracts all sorts of other wild life. The shape of the pond — whether formal or informal — can be selected to match the style of the rest of the garden and you can build one to almost any size you like.

There are two quite different ways of making a pond — either with a pre-formed rigid shell or with a flexible rubber or plastic liner. The pre-formed shells come in a variety of shapes — rectangular, round or irregular — and they range in size from about 3ft long to about 15ft (see Options). Flexible liners fit any shape, size or depth of hole and allow you to create your own design for the pond — and they're just as easy to install.

When choosing or designing a pond, bear in mind the needs of the stock you're planning to buy. Fish need a pond that's at least 18in deep, whereas many plants need much shallower water. A pond that has a shallow shelf and a deeper section in the middle is probably the best all-round choice.

The work of digging out the pond can be heavy so allow yourself plenty of time. Take time to plan ahead too, especially where you are going to put the soil you excavate. One solution is to build a rock garden somewhere else in the garden or at one side of the pool.

A poolside rock garden could be just the place to build a waterfall or cascade feature — bear this in mind when you are planning.

1 What the job involves

A successful pond is largely the result of careful planning and preparation as well as hard work.
You'll have to:
● decide on a location that avoids obstacles and underground pipes
● decide on the shape and size of the pond
● choose between a pre-formed pond and a flexible liner
● remove any turf from the area
● level the ground if necessary
● excavate the ground to the required depth and shape
● line the excavation with sand or newspaper to form a smooth bedding for the liner
● lay the liner and fill the pond
● edge the pond with paving stones
● stock with plants and fish

BEFORE YOU START

● when siting the pool, decide on a position where it can be drained without affecting the footings and foundations of any buildings.
● is the water table on any part of your garden high enough for a natural pond to be formed by excavating into it? If it is, a liner is not needed.
● make arrangements to dispose of any unwanted soil or debris.
● if you're thinking of adding a cascade or waterfall to the pool leave

CHECKLIST

Tools
spade, or pickaxe for hard ground
hose
level

Materials
wooden pegs and string
sand or damp newspaper
edging stones or paving slabs
bedding mix of one part cement
   to 20 parts sand

See Skills Guide
p. 132

room for this when you plan the position and shape of the pool.
● if you plan to use a flexible liner, work out what size you need to buy. The length of the liner should be the length of the pool plus twice the maximum depth. The width should equal the width of the pool plus twice the maximum depth.
● if you intend installing the pool on sloping ground, you'll have to cut back the higher side of the pool or build up the lower side. The top edge of the pool must be level.
● decide which color liner you prefer. Choices are usually black, stone, grey or blue. All are equally attractive but the blue makes the pond look more like a child's paddling pool.
● if you have particular plants in mind, check the depth of water they need. Draw a scale plan of the cross-sectional depths to work out the best arrangement.
● if you are considering a rigid liner, either of fiberglass or polyurethane, make sure there is one large enough for the pool you have in mind.

❗ WATCH OUT FOR

● cheap flexible liners made out of thin polyethylene. These become brittle in sunlight and in cold weather and can crack causing

If the ground slopes you'll have to build up the low side and cut away the high side so the perimeter of the pool is perfectly level

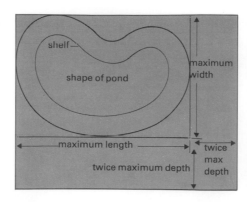

When calculating the size of the liner, add on twice the depth of the pool to the area you will cover

leaks. Thin liners are also easily damaged by plant roots and stones, and fish can nibble holes in them.
● flimsy rigid liners. These can crack, and repairs take time.
● an imbalance of plant life when stocking the pool. Never allow more than three fifths of the pool to be covered with plants and take care to choose plants which complement each other as well as your garden and are easy to look after.
● ponds that are too small or shallow. Ponds need a surface area of at least 40sq ft to maintain a balance between plant and fish life which helps keep the water clear. The depth should be at least 15in in the deepest part.
● hidden pipe or drain runs. If you are digging more than 12in deep near a house make sure you find out where services are buried to avoid damage to them. Local utilities will be able to give you this information.

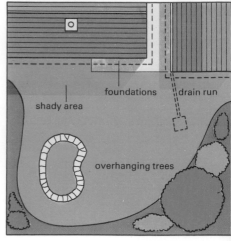

1. The pool should be away from overhanging trees, foundations, drains and too much shade

Exactly where you put your pond depends to a large extent on what is already in your yard.

Keep it away from overhanging trees and shrubs – dead leaves falling in autumn will soon fill up the pond and foul the water. Decaying leaves can also give off toxic gases which can be fatal to plants and fish. Even evergreens are best avoided as many of them carry leaves or berries which can poison fish.

Shade also encourages the growth of algae, turning the water a murky green, so make sure the pond benefits from plenty of sunlight – at least half a day's worth.

In colder areas of the country it's best to site the pond where it is protected from cold northerly and easterly winds. Alternatively, you can plant shrubs or build a low fence to protect its exposed sides and add yet more visual interest.

Natural ponds and pools are usually found in low-lying areas, so if you want a natural look choose this sort of location and an irregular shape for your pond.

It is easier to build the pond in a level area of garden. If you choose a sloping area you will have to level it first to fit a liner.

There are several advantages to locating it fairly close to the house. It is easy to reach with a hose when filling it, and it is near to a drain when emptying. The electricity

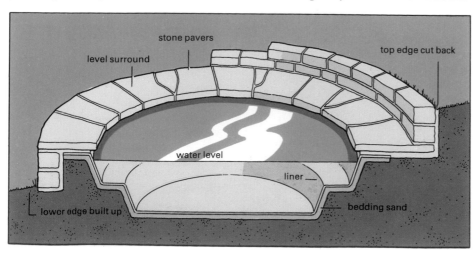

supply is also close by if you decide to add a fountain or pool lighting. And, perhaps more importantly, it is easier to keep an eye on children playing nearby. But do make sure the pond is away from footings or foundations which could be damaged by digging or if a leak develops.

Once you've chosen a location you can plan the best shape for the pond. For a regular pond, mark out the shape using stakes and string. For an irregular pond, try out different shapes and sizes by using a length of rope or garden hose as a marker for the outline of the pond. Push it into different shapes until you find one that looks right from different parts of the garden.

⭐ **TIP**

Even if you are buying a pre-formed pond you should try out different shapes first before selecting from the catalog to give you an idea of how they will look in situ.

Avoid any sharp bends or narrow inlets. A fairly rounded kidney shape or oval usually looks best. Once you've decided on the shape, mark around the outline with a spade or a trail of sand, then remove markers before you begin the next stage, of digging the hole.

2. Try out different shapes and positions using a garden hose or length of rope as a marker

1. Remove turf from the area and dig down to about 10in. The sides should slope gently

Digging out the hole is fairly straightforward. If you're setting the pond in grass, remove a 1ft to 2ft margin of turf from around the outside of the pond (to leave room for the edging) then mark round the outside again with the spade or sand and remove the rest of the turf from the inside of the pond line.

Check that the ground around the pond is fairly flat and level it if necessary then dig down to about 8 to 12in over the whole area. Mark out a shelf about 8–12in from the edge. Now dig out this central part to another 8 to 12in. This deeper trough is essential for fish.

Don't make the sides of the pond too steep or they may start to cave in. A slope out of about 4in is about right for a drop of 8 to 12in but soil types vary.

Tamp down the soil until it is quite firm and remove any sharp stones or roots. Then cover the soil with damp sand to a depth of about ½in as a bedding for the liner.

2. Use a datum stake in the center to check that the top edge is level in all directions

3. Mark out a shelf about 8in wide then dig out the central part to a further 10in

Measure the depth in cross-section *for the ideal size of the shelves and the slope of the sides*

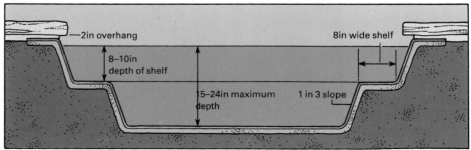

2in overhang — 8in wide shelf

8–10in depth of shelf

15–24in maximum depth — 1 in 3 slope

4 Fitting the liner

5 Laying edging

1. Lay the liner over the hole, weight down the edges and start to fill. Even out any creases

2. When the pond is full, trim off the excess liner leaving an overlap of 8–12in all the way around

Bed edging stones *on a sand and cement mix and let them overhang the edge of the pool by about 2in*

You should lay the liner as soon as the bedding is prepared, before the sand has a chance to dry out or the hole starts to fill with ground water.

Lay the liner centrally over the excavation and allow it to drape loosely in the hole. Weigh it around the edge with some heavy objects, such as bricks.

Run the garden hose into the center of the pond and start running in the water. The liner will gradually mold itself to the contours of the pond. You'll need to keep moving the weights as the liner is dragged inwards.

Keep a watch for any creases which may form and deal with them immediately. In some cases just going over the liner with a soft broom will help keep the pressure even. With larger creases or folds you'll have to pull the liner into shape and perhaps redistribute the weights.

Some creases are inevitable of course, the idea is just to keep them as small and evenly spaced as possible.

When the pond is full, trim the edge of the lining leaving overlaps at the sides of about 1ft.

Edging the pond is essential, both to protect the liner and hold it in place.

For a rectangular or square pond, the easiest and most common method is to use concrete paving slabs or irregular flagstone slabs. Just lay the stones in a firm bedding of sand mixed with one twentieth part cement laid around the edges of the pond and on top of the lining. The stones should overhang the pool by about 2in. Make sure that the overlap of the liner is tucked in tightly and held securely by the weight of the stones.

★ Easy way to prevent freezing

A pond heater keeps a small area of the pond ice free in low temperatures (this would be insufficient in very cold areas). This allows toxic gases to escape, protecting the fish. It is simply floated on the water and plugged into a low voltage electricity supply.

★ TIP

If any cement falls into the pond while you are constructing the edging, drain it and clean it out before refilling. Cement can be toxic to plant and fish life.

For ponds with more complicated shapes, check with the local garden center or building supplier to see if they have any shaped paving slabs to fit the outline of your pond or you can shape the slabs yourself.

Alternatively, use random paving or natural rocks and stones. It is possible to use turf for the edging, but it must be bedded on soil that's clear of the edge—don't allow it to overhang: it will grow back naturally in time.

6 Stock the pond

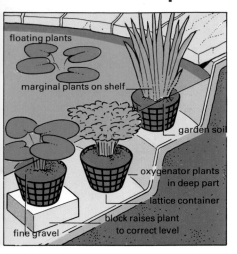

floating plants
marginal plants on shelf
garden soil
oxygenator plants in deep part
lattice container
block raises plant to correct level
fine gravel

Plants must be placed at the correct depth – stand them on bricks to make small adjustments

The newly-filled pond should be left empty for a few days for any harmful chemicals in the water to disperse before stocking it with plants and fish.

Oxygenator plants are essential if you plan to keep fish – your local garden center will be able to advise you. They keep the water clear and provide oxygen for the fish.

Buy one bunch of oxygenator plants for every 2sq ft of water surface area. Other plants to consider are colorful waterlilies and marginal plants such as bulrushes and irises.

Plant them in ordinary soil, as long as it is free from weedkiller or fertilizer, in lattice containers. Line the containers with burlap to stop the soil seeping into the water and cover the surface with fine gravel.

Add fish only when the oxygenators are established.

Do not overstock. As a guide, one square foot of surface area will support 2in of fish. So a pool 3ft by 6ft could support 36in of fish made up of 18 fish 2in long.

⭐ **TIP**

Put the bag containing the fish on the surface of the pond for about 30 minutes before releasing the fish so they can acclimatize.

7 Correct faults

If the water level drops in the summer this is probably due to evaporation. A drop of up to 2in a week is possible in very hot weather and the water level should be topped up from the hose.

If the water level drops more rapidly and evaporation is not the cause then there must be a hole in the liner. Allow the water level to reach its lowest point when the hole should be visible. Remove plants and fish as necessary. Do not pull the liner in an attempt to find the hole as this will cause more damage.

The puncture can be repaired in situ as most manufacturers supply puncture repair kits.

If the split in the liner is too large to be repaired or if the liner has generally deteriorated, you'll have to re-place it with a new one. Drain the pond, transferring the fish and plants to a temporary home – a series of buckets or old paddling pool – then lay the new liner over the old one. Don't remove the old liner as this will dislodge the soil. You'll have to lift up the edging to anchor the new liner. Refill the pool then replace the stock.

If the pond freezes over in the winter, then there is the danger that the fish will die. This is because gases given off by decaying vegetation become trapped under the ice and can be fatal to the fish. The solution is to install a pool heater which keeps a small area of the pool free from ice and lets the gases escape.

If falling leaves are a nuisance in autumn, or if you have trouble with cats trying to catch the fish, you can lay a net over the top of the pond. Plastic nets are available with a ¾in mesh, in sizes to fit most ponds and they are usually supplied with pegs to secure them into the ground.

If the pool is stocked but the water refuses to clear then buy an algicide. Several types are available, make sure you get a safe one.

Options

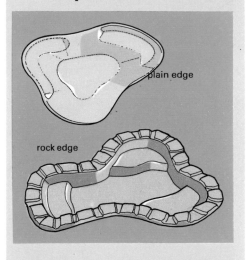

plain edge
rock edge

Pre-formed ponds are available in a variety of sizes, shapes, colors and finishes

Rigid pre-formed ponds are an alternative to flexible liners. Digging out the hole and installing them is just as easy. First take the liner and position it in the correct location. Take a handful of sand and let the sand dribble out slowly as you move your hand around the edge of the pond. This will trace out the outline of the pond.

Remove any turf then dig out the hole to the approximate depth and shape of the liner.

Place the liner in the hole and check that when it is level the top of the pond is just below soil level.

Remove any large stones from the area and tamp the soil down well. Using pieces of scrap lumber or brick, support the pool until it is level. Check this with a carpenter's level in several directions.

Remove the liner and fill around the supports with sand and bed the pool in until there is no movement when the pool is replaced. Check the level once more then back-fill around the sides of the liner with more sand. Fill the pool with water at the same rate as you back-fill round the sides so that it stays firmly in place.

Edge the pond in any of the ways described for the flexible liners, but take great care that the stones do not rest on the liner as the weight may cause it to crack – rigid liners are strong but brittle.

A Fountain and Waterfall

With a low-voltage, submersible electric pump and ready-made water feature, adding a waterfall or fountain to a pond is a straightforward job that will give your yard a visual focus and add immensely to your enjoyment of your outdoor living space.

The charm of running water has been known for centuries. Many of the great landscape architects of the past used it to design fabulous water gardens in which the sight and sound of waterfalls and fountains create an unrivalled air of peace and tranquility. Now, with the introduction of the electric water pump, almost anyone can share the experience.

Most water features are based on the scale of a garden pond – and if you keep fish, the circulation will also aerate and clean the water. But such is the compactness of modern designs that you can also create fountains around a miniature pool or even a large basin, making them ideal for use in a patio.

Waterfalls and cascades can both be bought premolded or home-built to your own design. Fountains range from self-contained jets with any number of sprays, to sculptured red basins and figures in plastic or artificial stone.

Most pumps are intended specifically for do it yourself use and are designed with safety in mind – so you don't need to worry about mixing electricity and water. The power can be from the main power supply or a low voltage transformer.

Pumps may be submersible or surface-mounted. The submersible type is easier to install, although it offers less output. Both come in a range of power ratings for different effects and sizes of feature.

1 What the job involves

Any water feature involves similar tasks, and even the most complicated – a waterfall – needs few tools and materials besides the pump and cascade. There are two parts to the job – installing the cascade itself and wiring up the pump. A ready-made fountain is even easier, since you just have to position the pump in the pool and then fit on the fountain head to finish off.

To add a waterfall to your pond you have to:
● Sketch out a plan based on either a ready-made cascade, or your own design
● choose a suitable pump to service the waterfall.
● prepare a soil base beside the pool for the cascade
● position the ready-molded cascade or form your own from pool liner material
● install the pump and pipework
● arrange a power supply and connect it to the pump
● finish off the area around the cascade with rocks and plants

CHECKLIST

Tools
spade
bucket
hose
level
trowel
wire strippers
screwdriver

Materials
hose clamps
sand
rocks/paving slabs
mortar for slabs
extension cord
weatherproof cable connector
plastic conduit and clips

See Skills Guide
pp. 132 and 136

BEFORE YOU START

● think about the design of your cascade. You need a header pool at the top, followed by the cascade itself, discharging into the pool at the bottom. Ready-made units may incorporate the header pool and cascade together, or you can combine separate units in a variety of ways. Space and the size of your pool should dictate the size of cascade, but remember that a long one will also need to be raised to a considerable height.

● choose the type of pump. The only real reason to choose a standard voltage powered pump is because your waterfall is so large that you need the extra output – for safety and ease of installation you should always choose a low-voltage type if this is powerful enough. Similarly, for all but very large installations, the submersible type is generally preferable.

● the power output you need depends on the size of your waterfall and whether you add a fountain. Ratings are given in Watts and in gallons or liters per hour. The flow rate depends on both the volume of the cascade and the 'head' (the vertical height to which the water is raised) so large falls need more powerful pumps. Low voltage types rarely exceed 70 Watts rated power, but their flow rate of around 150 gallons per hour at a head of 5ft is sufficient for most applications. If in doubt, most manufacturers supply both cascades and pumps and their brochures usually advise on suitable combinations. If you are adding a fountain, make sure that the pump is capable of supplying both high pressure/low volume for the fountain *and* low pressure/high volume for the fall.

● power supply cables to low voltage pumps are usually about 20 to 30ft between the pump and the

The power output of the pump determines both the maximum height or 'head' of water and the rate of flow. A flow adjuster on the pump directs water to the fountain or waterfall or both

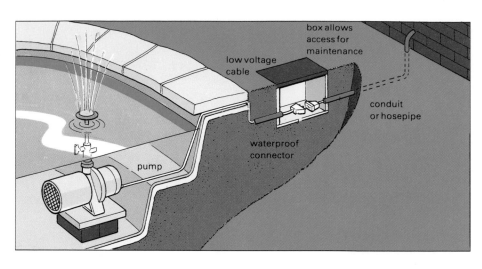

transformer. The transformer needs to be housed somewhere sheltered and dry, inside or in a shed and plugged into the main power supply. This means that you may either have to extend the cable between the pump and transformer (using a weather-proof cable connector) or arrange an outdoor power supply to a remote transformer.

! WATCH OUT FOR

● extending the low voltage cable from the transformer over about 36ft: this may result in a voltage drop causing a reduced pump output. In this case, you would have to opt for a more powerful pump or an outdoor power supply.

● home-made cascades: these generally need a higher powered

The transformer can normally be powered from the house circuit then a low voltage cable is run to the pump. Waterproof connectors must be used if the cable has to be extended outdoors

pump than their molded equivalents.

● too many plants: the pump needs to be placed in a free area of the base of the pond. The water is sucked in through a strainer and filter, but if the pond is heavily planted, you may need to cut back lilies and so on.

● the power supply: if you don't want to tie up an existing indoor socket permanently while the pump is in use, you may have to put in an extra socket outdoors. This must be a waterproof type incorporating a ground fault circuit interruption (GFCI) for safety.

2 Installing the cascade

1. Lay out the components and mark the position and size of the mound with stakes and string

2. Gradually build up the mound. Backfill with more soil, paying special attention to the edges

Rigid, molded cascade units only need a base of soil shaped roughly to the right profile. After positioning, you then pack more soil around the mold to support its contours and avoid any danger of it cracking when in use.

Some types of polyethylene molding are only semi-rigid. These need more careful soil and base preparation.

In either case, start by laying out the units roughly in place and mark out the profile with stakes and string – the stakes can be used to approximate the height, while the string shows the outline.

Remove any turf and set it aside for finishing off later. Then build up your pile of earth to the required height, trying the cascade units for fit as you go.

When you are reasonably satisfied, use a level to check that the units are level in both directions, and make sure that the lip of the bottom cascade is projecting properly over the pond.

With semi-rigid cascades, now go over the earth mound and check that it is free from any stones or other projections. Compact the earth, then spread a layer of sand over it to a depth of about ½in to provide a smooth bed. Fiberglass cascades do not need this extra step.

Lay the cascade in place and backfill under and around it with more

3. Fill the header pool and cascade with water to hold them in position while you pack in the filling

sifted earth or sand, packing it in hard, especially underneath the shelves which may sag if they are not fully supported.

⭐ **TIP**

If you fill the pools of the cascade with a little water, the extra weight will hold the unit in position while you backfill.

Once your cascade is in place, you are ready to run in the supply hose from the pump. Do this before adding the finishing touches around the edges of the mound.

3 The pump

It should take only minutes to assemble the pump and install it according to the manufacturer's instructions.

The pump will be supplied with the power cable already wired in, but you may have to add the hose for the supply to the header pool, and the inlet filter, plus the fountain head if you have chosen to use one. The parts for the fountain head simply push-fit together.

Hoses usually just push into place, but you can add hose clamps for extra security – don't overtighten these onto plastic in case you crack it. Make sure your hose is over the required length and don't cut it yet – wait until you have finally laid it in position.

1. Assemble the fountain head – the parts push-fit together – and add the fountain jet at the top

2. Fit the fountain head to the pump, push on the hose then add the filter assembly

3. Position the pump making sure that the fountain is just above water level and the inlet is free

4. The hose to the waterfall should be buried in the mound to conceal it, then cut to length

⭐ **TIP**

Warm the end of the hose in hot water to make it slip on easily and improve the seal.

Put the pump below the water on a firm, level surface like a stone slab. If you are using a fountain head, this must just project above the surface of the water.

Run the waterfall hose out of the pool where it will not show – such as under the lip of the cascade. Take it to the header pool, cut it to the right length, then conceal the remaining pipe in the mound.

1. Run the cable in conduit or plastic pipe and bury it to protect it from accidental damage

A low voltage cable does not constitute a hazard, but you must still lay it so it is safe from damage.
This means either burying it or sheathing it in conduit.

⭐ **TIP**

The wiring will be inaccessible once installed, so test it in a 'dry run' first.

Choose the most direct route from the pump to the transformer which should be kept dry and sheltered.

With this ·in mind, lay out your cable. Any joins must be with a weatherproof connector, and left accessible for maintenance. The extension must be in heavy-duty, insulated and sheathed cable.

Trail the pump cable across the bottom of the pond to the edge under one of the border slabs, from where it can be run underground. When you are burying the cable, make the trench at least 20in deep, to protect it from digging.

Where the cable is to run along a wall, feed it through a length of conduit, and screw the conduit in place.

The cable has only two wires, which can be connected to the transformer either way round. Bare the ends and connect them to the two *low-voltage* terminals.

Add rocks and plants *so the molded cascade blends in naturally with the surroundings*

With your new water feature fully functional, the final step is to give the edges a natural appearance.
The edges of molded cascades are finished with natural-looking simulated rocks – help complete the illusion by adding some real stone around them.

⭐ **TIP**

Place pieces of stone in the header pool to conceal the pipe and spread the water flow, giving a more natural effect.

Finally, add rockery plants between the stones, and establish some aquatic plants in the larger pools of the cascade itself.

⭐ *Safer power*

Low voltage pumps are a safer way to power a water feature. But if you have to take any standard voltage power supply into the garden you need additional protection.

One of the easiest and cheapest ways to do this is to provide the power via a plug which incorporates a ground fault circuit interruption (GFCI).

If there is a fault in the appliance, or the power cable is accidentally cut, the device will cut off the electric supply instantly.

Climbing Frame

It's often a problem finding a safe area for adventurous children to play and explore, but this climbing frame and tree house offers relative safety and a chance to exercise a childish imagination.

You don't need a tree in your yard to be able to build this project as a climbing frame, but it does help – even though the structure's not anchored to the trunk. A tree is an invitation to play and explore, so build a frame around it and you've got a sturdy frame and a tree house in one. There's no need for cross bracing – which would damage the

tree – and there is little risk of injury to your children.

The design is infinitely adaptable – as it must be – and based on lumber sizes and component spacings to make it rigid, durable, yet exciting enough to exercise your imagination and your children.

The frame is easy to construct and easy to adapt using the treated lumber and ½in exterior C grade plywood that's specified in the checklist. Plywood side braces strengthen the frame and are rigid enough to climb up. Moveable sections allow children to explore different arrangements, yet lock into place for safety.

Though it's adaptable, there are limits you must observe. Follow the assembly plan and use the sizes of lumber and plywood specified: adapt only the lengths you need to fit around your tree. Don't alter the critical dimensions of height and component spacings and the structure will be safe and solid. For most other lengths you can use a 'direct measure' principle and cut components of similar length at the same time. Throughout, you'll find a portable workbench, power tools and an extension cord are a must. The checklist above covers the amount of material used on this project and this particular tree – anything left over on yours can be used for all sorts of odds and ends – or to create an additional 'den' within the main levels of the frame.

TREE HOUSE AND FRAME DESIGN

MAKE THE SIDE FRAMES

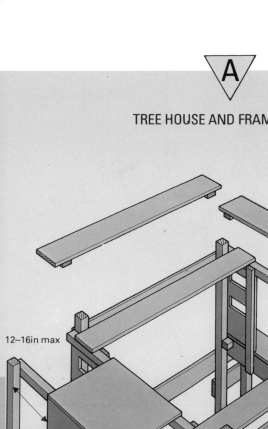

loose connecting boards

connecting board

12–16in max

steps

side assembly

steps

Measure diagonals to check uprights are parallel

4 × 4 softwood

8in wide plywood

steps

Check frames side-by-side for uniformity

32in max

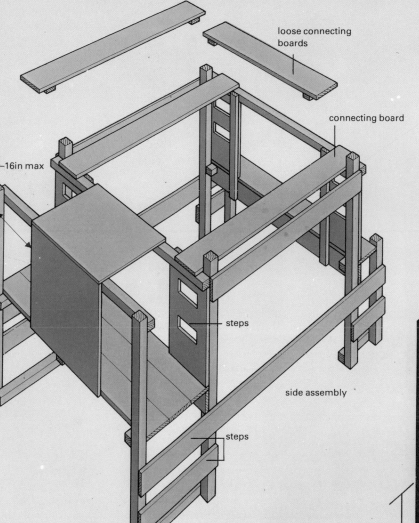

The structure consists of two identical side frame assemblies which carry the steps and supports for the two longer floors or levels. The uprights closest to the trunk are the longest and shouldn't be made higher than 7ft. Exterior grade plywood acts as a brace at critical points while softwood boards serve for floors or as optional loose connecting boards (which lock into place). Pay attention to the step heights – they may need altering to suit the size of the smallest child likely to use the frame, otherwise make each step a maximum of 16in high.

With such a structure, it's important to prevent 'racking' out of square. Aim to make everything level and upright and attach the plywood braces at the places and with the fastenings shown. Some components can be nailed, others screwed, yet others must be counterbored and screwed.

Make the central uprights a maximum of 84in, the shortest at 44in high. Nail joints at first until all is square, then drill and screw for strength.

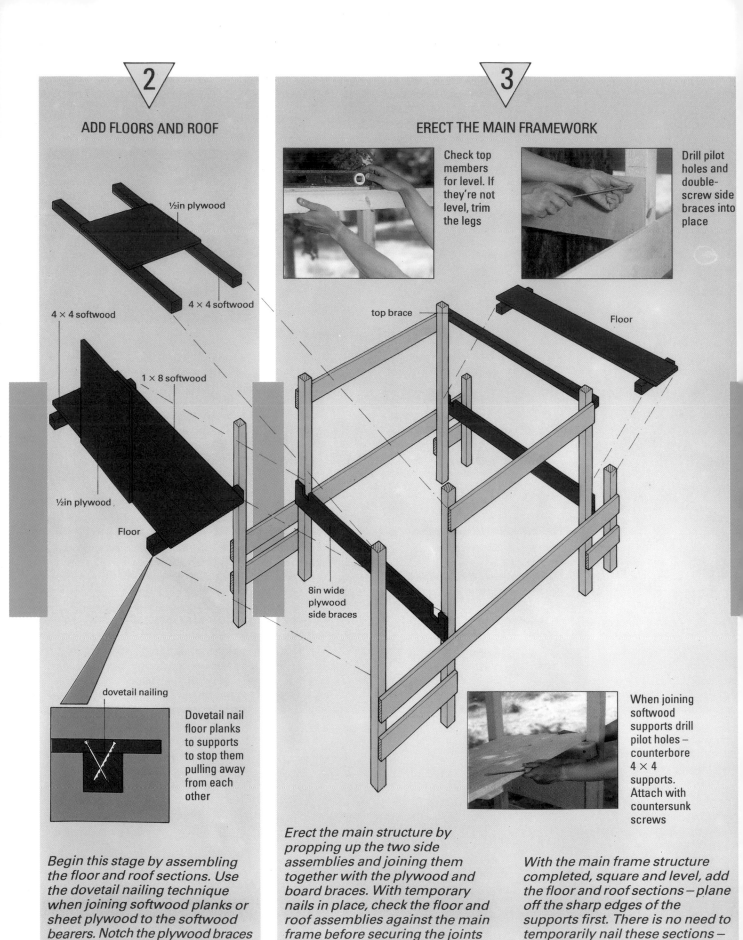

½in plywood

4 × 4 softwood

4 × 4 softwood

1 × 8 softwood

½in plywood

Floor

dovetail nailing

Dovetail nail floor planks to supports to stop them pulling away from each other

Check top members for level. If they're not level, trim the legs

Drill pilot holes and double-screw side braces into place

top brace

Floor

8in wide plywood side braces

When joining softwood supports drill pilot holes – counterbore 4 × 4 supports. Attach with countersunk screws

Begin this stage by assembling the floor and roof sections. Use the dovetail nailing technique when joining softwood planks or sheet plywood to the softwood bearers. Notch the plywood braces that support the floor bearers.

Erect the main structure by propping up the two side assemblies and joining them together with the plywood and board braces. With temporary nails in place, check the floor and roof assemblies against the main frame before securing the joints with counterbored 4in screws.

With the main frame structure completed, square and level, add the floor and roof sections – plane off the sharp edges of the supports first. There is no need to temporarily nail these sections – drill pilot holes before securing.

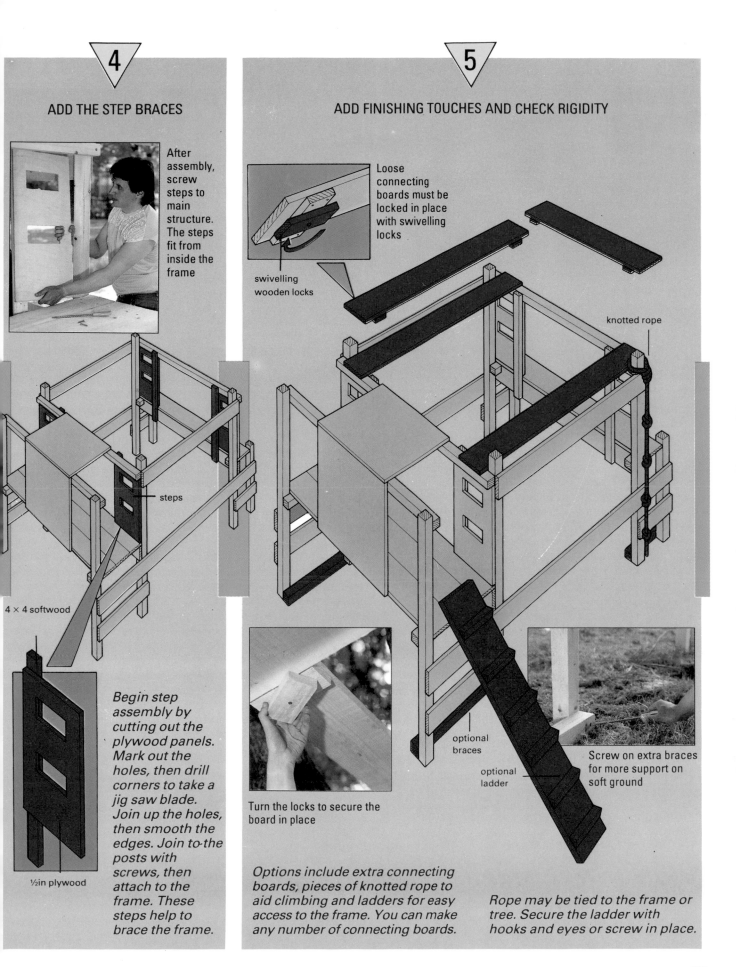

4

ADD THE STEP BRACES

After assembly, screw steps to main structure. The steps fit from inside the frame

4 × 4 softwood

steps

½in plywood

Begin step assembly by cutting out the plywood panels. Mark out the holes, then drill corners to take a jig saw blade. Join up the holes, then smooth the edges. Join to the posts with screws, then attach to the frame. These steps help to brace the frame.

5

ADD FINISHING TOUCHES AND CHECK RIGIDITY

Loose connecting boards must be locked in place with swivelling locks

swivelling wooden locks

knotted rope

optional braces

optional ladder

Turn the locks to secure the board in place

Screw on extra braces for more support on soft ground

Options include extra connecting boards, pieces of knotted rope to aid climbing and ladders for easy access to the frame. You can make any number of connecting boards.

Rope may be tied to the frame or tree. Secure the ladder with hooks and eyes or screw in place.

Patio Furniture

When spring is in the air, thoughts turn from keeping warm to enjoying the outside. With this bench and table you can sit outside during the milder weather and, when it becomes too cold again, you can simply leave the furniture where it is.

Patio furniture can be cumbersome and unattractive and, worse still, it's often not built to last. The matching seat and table pictured here is both elegant and durable and, as it can be made in softwood treated with preservative, it's not expensive.

Taking inspiration from the Orient, the design features clean lines and a geometric lattice resulting in a duo decorative enough to grace a garden, patio or sunspace. And although the furniture looks professionally made, it's well within the capabilities of the amateur. Simply follow the instructions with care, making sure that you measure and cut the components accurately and spend time on the rounded armrests and seat rails.

CHECKLIST

Tools and Materials
softwood or cedar
¼in dowels
woodworking glue
jigsaw or saber saw and backsaw
dowelling bit and jig
try square and measure
string and furniture clamps
screws and nails
screwdriver and hammer
wood preservative

⬜ See Skills Guide pp. 112, 116, 117, 120 and 121

THE FURNITURE'S DESIGN

The attractive outdoor bench is made exclusively from finished softwood which is treated with a wood preservative to make it durable enough for outside use. Red cedar or teak is more suitable, but much more costly. Sturdy 2 × 3 and 2 × 2 sections make up the basic framework, while the seat rails and decorative lattices are 1 × 3 and 2 × 2 respectively.

It's designed to be assembled in easy stages, using only simple dowel joints. To make sure that it remains perfectly in square, it's

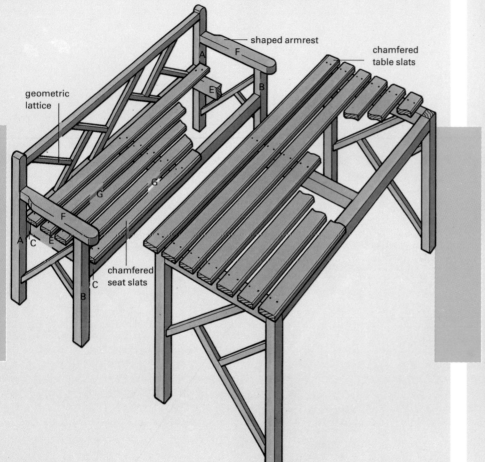

shaped armrest

chamfered table slats

geometric lattice

chamfered seat slats

important to allow the joints to set at each stage before moving on to the next.

Assembly begins with constructing the front and back frames. The decorative lattice is then set into the back frame before it is attached to the front one with a series of cross-rails. The armrests, seat slats and end lattices complete the assembly.

The table, designed to complement the bench, employs the same techniques, but is easier to build. The framework, comprising 4 legs, 3 cross-rails and 2 long-rails, can be assembled in one operation (provided that clamps are used to keep the structure rigid while the glue sets). The table slots can then be screwed in place. Finally, decorative leg lattices to match those on the back and ends of the bench are added. Remember you can reduce the height if you wish.

1

CUT SEAT COMPONENTS

Shape the armrests (F) by cutting straight along the marked lines with a jigsaw. Sand edges smooth

A×2 B×2 C×2 D×1 G×5

E×3 F×2

A = 29×2×2in
B = 22×2×2in
C = 48×2×3in
D = 48×2×2in
E = 14×2×3in
F = 18×2×4in
G = 48×1×3in

Following the cutting plan and chart above, prepare the main components for the garden seat. Cut the shaped parts – the uprights in the back frame (A) and the armrests (F) – to the sizes indicated then shape them individually before putting them together. Outline the shaping, then cut straight through the wood using a jigsaw or bandsaw. Sand the edges until they are rounded and smooth to the touch.

MAKE THE SEAT FRAMES

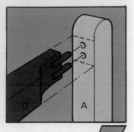

Assemble the front and back frames using 3 dowels for joints between parts C, B and A, and 2 for parts D and A

back frame

To stop the frames from twisting while the glue dries, lay them flat and use wedges to hold them rigid

Mark the positions for parts C 13in from the bottom of parts A and B, and for part D 1in from the top of each A. Make the dowel holes using a jig. Test fit then glue and wedge tight.

ASSEMBLE THE LATTICE

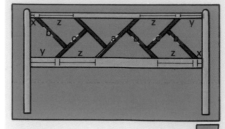

a = 19in

b = 11½in

c = 15in

x = 1in

y = 5in

z = 10in

miter cut ends

Assemble the lattice by glueing the dowels in place and position it while the glue is wet. Adjust its position and trim to fit if necessary then glue and nail the ends to the back frame

90° butt joint

Cut the lattice parts from 2 × 2 lumber, making 45 degree miter cuts to the ends that will meet the frame. Lay it out and mark and make dowel holes. Test fit, adjust, then secure the lattice.

ASSEMBLE THE CARCASE

To ensure the carcase stays in shape, secure it with string or furniture clamps until the glue has dried

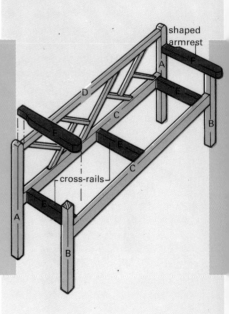

shaped armrest

cross-rails

Position the armrests (F) then mark and make dowel holes for connecting into the top of B and side of A

Mark joint positions for the cross-rails (E). Set one 1in in from each end of C and the other midway between. Connect them using 2 dowels per joint, then clamp until set. Add the armrests.

5

FINISH THE BENCH

For a neat finish, chamfer the edges of the seat slats (G) with a large plane

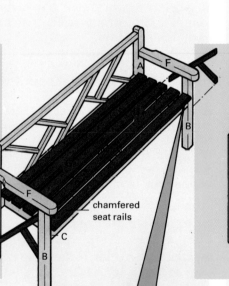

chamfered seat rails

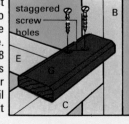

Set the first slat to overhang the front frame. Use 2 1¼in No. 8 zinc or brass screws for each cross-rail joint

staggered screw holes

Space the seat slats evenly over the carcase, then screw them in place. Cut 2 lattice parts 19in and 8½in long for each end and position as before – the longer part 2in from under the armrest.

6

MAKE THE TABLE FRAME

Add the table cross-rails (J) to parts H and I using 3 dowels per joint. Use 2 dowels for the remaining carcase joints

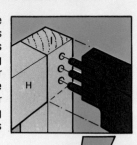

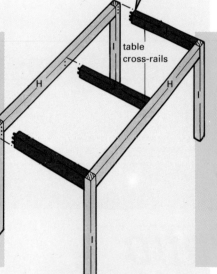

table cross-rails

To make a table to match the bench, you'll need a basic framework of 3 20 × 3 × 2in cross-rails (J), 2 49 × 3 × 2in long-rails (H), and 4 28 × 2 × 2in legs (I). Assemble the framework as before using 3 dowels to connect the cross-rails (J) to the legs and long-rails, and 2 for the joints between the long-rails and the legs. It's important to stagger the dowel positions when joining the long-rails and cross-rails to the legs.

7

FINISH THE TABLE

To prevent wood decay due to water damage, paint the furniture with an exterior wood preservative and colorant

m = 1½in
o = 22in
p = 18½in
q = 14½in
r = 11in

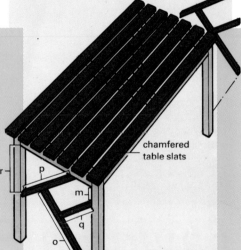

chamfered table slats

To finish the table, first cut 7 slats 54in long, using 1 × 3 board as before. Chamfer the edges with a plane, then space the slats evenly over the carcase with an overhang on all edges. Connect them with 2 screws for each joint. Cut the lattice parts for each end, using the measurements above, and secure them in place. Prepare the seat and table for use by treating the wood with a preservative. Follow the manufacturer's instructions as to the number of coats required.

Laying a Patio

A paved patio is a stepping stone between house and yard, providing somewhere to sit, eat out or sunbathe on sunny days and giving children a firm outdoor play area. In short it is the perfect center for outdoor living during times of warm weather.

Creating a patio is a straightforward and highly satisfying outdoor home improvement project. The job is not particularly difficult, so amateur builders need not be daunted – in fact, it's sometimes possible to get away without even having to mix up any mortar. What's more, the finished job can transform your property and allow you to enjoy your yard to the full, whether it's half

an acre of greenery or just a lawn the size of a postage stamp.

It's easiest to build a patio if you've got a flat site, but if yours slopes some simple earth-retaining walls can easily be incorporated into the design, and you then have the opportunity to experiment with different levels. Remember also that you don't have to have your patio at the back of the house; if space permits, put it at the side to catch the best of the sun, or even at the far end of your yard.

There is a wide range of paving materials available in many different surface textures and colors, so it will be easy to make the patio match the style of your house, and you need little in the way of tools and special equipment to do a first-class job.

1 What the job involves

The job of paving a patio divides neatly into two major parts. The most important is the initial planning; if that is well done, the construction work will proceed quickly and easily. As far as the actual building work is concerned, you have to:
● choose and estimate the materials you will use to build it
● decide how you're going to bed the slabs – on sand or in mortar
● prepare the site, including laying foundations for any walls that are part of the scheme
● build earth-retaining walls if necessary and any other features, such as planters and steps between different levels
● spread a uniform layer of sand to receive the slabs, or mix up a quantity of bedding mortar
● lay the paving slabs themselves
● point between the slabs, if they are bedded in mortar.

BEFORE YOU START

● plan the position of the patio with care so that it catches the maximum sunlight and also, if possible, affords a pleasant view.
● decide on its overall size. It must be big enough to accommodate outdoor furniture, plus perhaps a children's sandbox, some plant tubs and a space for the barbecue.
● think about drainage, especially if the yard rises away from the house. You may need to incorporate a gully and dry well in the construction.
● try to keep the level of the patio at least 6in below the threshold of the doors to avoid debris blowing into the house.
● sketch out a scale plan to indicate the positions of features such as planters, retaining walls and steps between different levels
● estimate your materials carefully. In particular, you have to decide at this stage whether

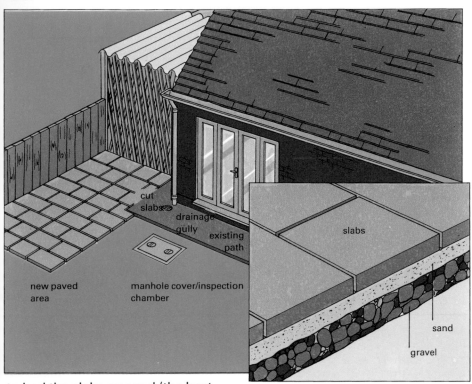

cut
slabs

drainage
gully

existing
path

new paved
area

manhole cover/inspection
chamber

slabs

sand

gravel

to bed the slabs on sand (the best choice on a virgin site) or mortar (if you're paving over concrete).
● work out how you will reach the patio from the house. You may want to convert a window to French or sliding patio doors, for example.
● reserve any tools you may need to rent for the job – a heavy duty wheelbarrow, for example, or an angle grinder if you anticipate having to cut a lot of the slabs down to size.

Pick a site that gets the sun and lay paving slabs on a level bed of sand over gravel

! WATCH OUT FOR

● well-established trees or shrubs that are to be paved around. An opening of at least 12in diameter should be left unpaved around the trunks, to guarantee a good supply of water to the roots
● recently dug up ground. This could subside after the paving has been put down, causing an uneven surface on which puddles will collect. An even surface is also essential for furniture to stand on without wobbling.

CHECKLIST

Tools
spade
wheelbarrow
level
long wooden straightedge
garden rake
wide cold chisel and club hammer
angle grinder (optional)
trowel

Materials
paving slabs
sand
gravel
mortar
stakes and string
spacers
concrete for wall foundations
bricks or blocks for walls

See Skills Guide pp. 123, 132 plus 124–128, 135 and 136 if walls are required.

2 Plan layout

Careful planning is essential, both to help you estimate materials accurately and to smooth the progress of the construction. Even if your patio is to be just a simple rectangle on a perfectly level site, it is worth measuring the site accurately – if only so that you can avoid having to cut slabs or bricks to size. If your plan is more complicated, or you will be working on different levels, detailed drawings are a must.

Begin by choosing your paving materials, and find out what sizes are available. Most slabs are square but with some ranges – especially hexagonal ones – you can obtain special half-slabs to finish off the edges neatly.

Next make a scale drawing of the proposed patio area, so that you can work out how many slabs will be required. It's best to use squared paper for this and to adopt a scale no smaller than ¼in:1ft. If you are using slabs with different colors, draw in the pattern on the plan.

If you are incorporating walls and steps in your design, choose what blocks to use and find out what sizes are available. Make note of the extra materials you will need for retaining walls and steps.

Where a sloping site is involved, you'll also need sectional drawings that show the precise positions of retaining walls, steps linking different levels and so on.

1. Working from a scale plan of the patio, measure and mark out the site with stakes and string.

3 Estimate materials

You can now use your drawings to work out precisely how many bricks or paving slabs will be needed, and also what quantities of sand, mortar, gravel and any walling materials to order.

Start by adding up the number of slabs, counting any cut slabs on the plan as whole ones, and add about 5 per cent to the total to allow for breakages during cutting and laying. If mixed colors or textures are being used, count each one up separately from your drawing.

Next, estimate the numbers of blocks or bricks that will be needed for any walls you will be building. The simplest way of doing this for a wall built in running bond is to calculate the area of walling (length × height) and divide it by the face area of an individual block or brick. So for standard bricks measuring 8 × 2¾in with a face area of 18sq in, one square yard (1296sq in) of wall will require 1296 ÷ 18 = approximately 72 bricks. A wall 7½in thick will need twice as many bricks.

If you are planning to use a sand bed for the slabs, measure the patio area in square yards and multiply by ¹⁄₁₂ to give the volume of sand that will be required in cubic yards if you are using a base of 3in. Round the answer up to the nearest 9cu ft – the smallest unit you can order from most suppliers.

The factor of ¹⁄₁₂ means a nominal sand thickness of 3in; the bed actually need be no thicker than 2in overall but an allowance must be made for the inevitable dips in the sub-soil that will be left once the site has been levelled.

For laying bricks and walling blocks, and for bedding slabs in mortar, you should use 1 part masonry cement (which contains the right amount of lime and some sand) to 3 parts sand. However if you are planning to use a lot of mortar it is cheaper to mix your own using cement lime and sand. To mix cement-lime mortar mix 1 part cement to ½ part lime and 4½ parts sand. Hydrated lime is added to the mixture dry however you must add water to quicklime before adding it to the mixture. To mix the mortar properly, first mix the cement and sand thoroughly and then add the lime and mix all the ingredients again. Slowly add water to the mixture until it is smooth and a consistent color throughout the mixture.

A combination of 3 bags masonry cement and 9 cubic feet of sand should produce enough mortar to lay 30 slabs using the '5-dot' method, or approximately 1¾sq yds of paving over a continuous mortar bed 1in thick.

For foundations for walls, use a concrete mix of 1 part cement to 3 parts fine aggregate and 4 parts coarse aggregate. Five bags of cement plus 35cu ft of aggregate yield 35cu ft of concrete, as the cement merely fills in the gaps between the aggregate particles, rather than adding to the total volume.

⭐ **TIP**

If you have to in-fill the site of the patio, use mixed aggregate. Coarse gravel is difficult to pack down thoroughly without leaving voids and the lumps make it hard to drive in pegs for setting out your levels.

Don't forget to include ancillary items such as gullies and drain pipes when ordering materials.

Make sure you are ready for the

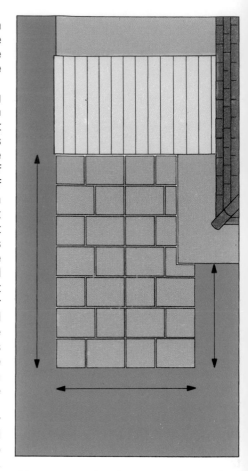

Use your scale plan to work out what materials you need. Count cut slabs as whole ones.

delivery of the materials. The truck will dump your sand on your driveway so have a team of friends lined up to help move it to near the patio site. Store cement under cover and off the ground, so that it doesn't get damp. Check the paving slabs or bricks for damage as they are unloaded, and send back any that are found to be chipped or cracked.

If materials have to be stacked in the road, keep piles and stacks neat and ensure that they are lit at night.

1. Store the slabs until needed by standing them on wooden strips and leaning them against a wall.

⭐ **TIP**

Stack the slabs on edge, leaning against a wall and standing on scrap strips of wood, to protect them from damage until you are ready to lay them.

4 Prepare the site

With all the planning and estimating complete and the materials ordered, begin the actual construction work.

If you are working on a virgin site, the first job is to clear it of all vegetation, except trees and shrubs that will be paved round. Save the topsoil for use somewhere else.

The next job is to set the patio level using datum stakes. For a patio adjoining the house, drive in a 1ft long stake next to the house wall, just outside the left-hand edge of the patio, and set its top at least 6in below the level of the door threshold. Set another stake at the other edge, and add intermediate stakes at 4ft intervals in between. Check with a level and straight board that all the stake tops are level. These stakes provide a reference point for levels throughout the job, and the two outer stakes are left in place until laying is complete.

You can now excavate the site. On firm subsoil that has not recently been disturbed, dig to a depth of around 6in, then lay about 3in of gravel or finely crushed stone and tamp it down well with something like a heavy fence post. If you find any soft spots, dig down until you reach solid subsoil and pack the hollows with well-compacted mixed aggregate.

Drive in some more stakes across the site at 4ft intervals, setting their tops to give a slight fall away from the house – about 1in in 10ft will be adequate.

If a gully and drywell are needed to drain the patio area, dig out the trench next and position the gully itself on a concrete base with its drain cover level with the tops of the datum stakes. Lay the pipe run to the site of the drywell.

Now spread the sand bed across the patio site, working on one 'bay' between the datum stakes at a time. Use your tamping beam on edge to pack the sand down until it is level with the tops of the stakes. Continue until the whole patio area is covered and then re-check the levels carefully.

If your patio is on several levels, excavate and stake out each one separately, and check that the drop from one level to the next is correct. Consider the number of steps between levels, each step should have a tread of at least 11in and a riser of no more than 7½in. Now is also the time to excavate and lay foundations for any earth-retaining walls required in the plan.

★ TIP

Once you have completed this stage, rope off the area to prevent anyone walking on the sand. Remind your children that it is not a new play area!

5 Lay the slabs

That's all the difficult preliminary work done. Now you can start on the rewarding part of the job – actually laying the paving.

It's best to lay the first row of slabs one row away from the house wall, so that you can set them level with the row of datum stakes. The row next to the wall can be laid at the end of the job. Set each slab in position, tamp it down gently using the handle of your club hammer and check that it is level with the datum peg, using a level and straightedge. Then lay the next slab, either butted tight against the first one or set a small distance away from it with small hardboard or plywood spacers.

As you lay further slabs, add or remove sand underneath to make sure each one is flush with its neighbour. Refer to the other stakes further away from the house to check that you are maintaining the desired fall.

Remove stakes from within the patio area as you reach them, checking your levels with the perimeter pegs as you complete each row. Continue until all the whole slabs have been laid, then check the overall level and fall once again.

If you have to cut slabs, mark the cutting line and score it with a wide cold chisel. Then use the chisel with a club hammer to cut slowly along the line, with the slab resting on the sand bed. Set the cut piece in place in the same way as the whole slabs.

1. Check the tops of the stakes with a level, remembering to allow a slight slope for drainage.

2. Fill any hollows with well compacted gravel or rubble laid on the sub-soil, then spread the sand.

1. Tap slabs down with the club hammer's butt, ensuring they are level and flush with each other.

At the edge of the paved area, make sure that the sand bed does not subside by adding a little extra sand before you bed in the last slabs. It may be necessary to use some form of temporary edge support to keep the bed in place.

⭐ **TIP**

If you have a lot of awkward cutting to do, or you find that the slabs won't break cleanly using the chisel and club hammer, it's best to rent an angle grinder and to saw the slabs to size. You get a perfect cut every time, with the minimum of wastage. An angle grinder is particularly useful where you have to cut slabs to fit around a drain, or round projections from the house wall such as downspouts.

The cheapest paving slabs are made from cast concrete containing solid aggregate rather than hydraulically compressed crushed rock, and they are almost impossible to cut cleanly by any method. Furthermore, even if the 'cut' edge is fairly straight it will leave coarse aggregate exposed. It is best to avoid this type unless only whole slabs will be laid.

If you are laying slabs on an existing concrete base, you can bed each one on five dabs of mortar or on a continuous mortar bed about 1in

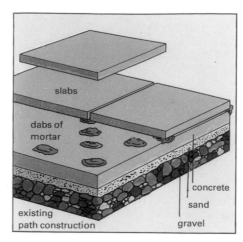

For a firmer support, lay slabs on five dabs of mortar – one at each corner and one in the middle.

thick. With the continuous bed, the gaps between the slabs are then pointed with mortar, after removing the spacers. With the '5-dot' method, traditional pointing is not very effective, and it is often better to butt the slabs tightly together and then to brush dry sand (or sand mixed with cement) into the gaps.

Always use a continuous bed of mortar for laying any slabs that form flights of steps. It is not safe to rely on their weight to keep them in place on a sand bed. Make sure, too, that each tread slopes slightly towards its front edge, so that rainwater drains quickly off the step. It is also worth using the '5-spot' mortar method where you are laying slabs in 'heavy-traffic' areas (outside the kitchen door, for example). Where the paving must cope with very heavy loads, lay it on a continuous mortar bed over a concrete slab foundation.

⭐ **TIP**

For traditional pointing, use mortar that is very dry to avoid staining the slabs. Chop it well into the gaps and recess it slightly with a piece of scrap wood, to create drainage channels for rainwater before sweeping over with a soft brush. Where mortar pointing isn't needed, consider using soil seeded with suitably hardy plants.

2. *An angle grinder is useful if the patio requires a lot of awkward cut paving slabs.*

6 Correct faults

If you find that any slabs are sitting proud of their neighbors, or are showing signs of subsiding, simply pry them up with your wide cold chisel and add or remove sand from underneath to bring them back to the correct level.

If you have smeared pointing mortar onto the face of the slabs, try to scrub it off with water before it has a chance to set; you can always re-point the joint later when the slabs have dried. If it has set, the best method of removing it is with a commercial stone cleaner. Note that these are based on hydrochloric acid, so they should be used with great care and strictly in accordance with the maker's instructions.

If you find moss and lichen starting to grow on the surface of the slabs, brush on a commercial moss killer. This will help to prevent regrowth, although further applications may be necessary if the patio is frequently damp and receives little direct sun.

If laying slabs on a 'virgin' weed infested site, spray the area with a proprietary long-acting weed killer before putting down the sand bed. You can also lay a sheet of heavy black plastic under the sand bed to discourage weed growth. This will prevent weed seedlings growing up beneath and between the new slabs.

1. *Lever up slabs that aren't flush with their neighbors and add or remove sand before relaying them.*

Installing New Patio Doors

Sliding patio doors, which are available in a wide variety of sizes, materials and finishes, provide the perfect link between the inside of your home and your outdoor living space. If they are manufactured with energy efficient sealed double glazed units, they are practical even in very cold climates.

Modern sliding patio doors can greatly improve access between your house and yard, bringing more light to your living room and giving you a more attractive view of your yard and the great outdoors – much more than a single glazed door or a window can offer. Because they're double-glazed you don't suffer enormous heat losses in cold weather, and models with solar control glass prevent the room from overheating in summer. Frames with thermal breaks greatly reduce the condensation problems early models suffered from, and improved locks and other hardware make them an effective barrier against burglars. And installing the doors within an existing opening is surprisingly easy.

A wide range of widths, arrangements – of two, three or four doors – and styles – plain, period or leaded – makes it easy to choose a model to suit your house. There's a choice of finishes too, ranging from anodized aluminum to white, gold, bronze and black, plus frames in wood or vinyl as an alternative to aluminum. Hardwood sub-frames complement the doors themselves to guarantee long life.

In another Project you'll see how to make the most of your patio doors by constructing a raised wooden sundeck as an attractive alternative to a paved patio.

1 What the job involves

Installing patio doors is relatively simple, provided that you plan everything carefully in advance and check your work for accuracy at every stage. Precise measurements and installation are vital if your new doors are going to operate smoothly and be completely weatherproof. To install them you have to follow a precise sequence.

● Measure the opening's height and width accurately.

● Choose a door and frame that closely matches the opening size – especially on width.

● External walls are always bearing walls and cannot be altered without affecting the structure of the house.

CHECKLIST

Tools
club hammer
narrow and wide cold chisel
hacksaw
screwdrivers
hand saw
crowbar
angle grinder (rented)
electric drill
assorted twist and masonry bits
measuring tape
try square
level
trowel
paint brush

Materials
woodscrews and wall plugs or
 ⅜in steel anchor bolts
waterproof wood adhesive
vapor barrier
caulking
mortar
varnish or preservative stain

See Skills Guide p. 138

Do not extend the width of opening. Remove the existing doors and frame. If you have French doors or just a conventional window frame, you may also have to remove some masonry too.

Put in a new wooden sub-frame within the opening, and ensure continuity of the vapor barrier around the opening.

Put in the new sub-frame and secure it to the rough framing.

Install the fixed and sliding panels and adjust their alignment.

Add locks and other accessories.

Repair any damage to the wall surface and finish off the new frame indoors and on the outside.

Dispose of the old frames and the old doors.

BEFORE YOU START

double-check dimensions carefully – a mistake could be expensive, and time-consuming, to rectify. Take measurements from one side of the opening to the other at several points with a steel tape – chipping away stucco outside if necessary to enable you to see where the frame actually begins and ends. Measure to the nearest $\frac{1}{16}$in for greater accuracy.

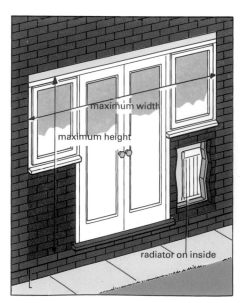

Measure the total height and width of the opening and watch out for obstructions such as a radiator

● remember to make allowances for the thickness of the sub-frame.
● check the components of the kit and count all the parts to make sure everything has been delivered and is undamaged.
● clear the room where the doors are being installed as much as possible – cover over carpets, take down curtains and cover furniture you can't move with dust sheets.
● clear enough space outside – on the patio or lawn – so you can lay out and assemble the sub-frame and frame, and lay down some plastic sheeting if the ground is damp.
● get someone fairly strong to help you lift the panels – they're surprisingly heavy.

! WATCH OUT FOR

● heating ducts, pipework and electric cables on the inside of wall sections you will be removing. Re-route them before you start.
● hidden fastenings holding the old frames in place: make sure you've removed or cut through them all around the opening.
● cavity walls: the flashing at the bottom of a cavity wall directs moisture which collects in the cavity to the weep holes and out onto the ground. This flashing needs to be continuous and may have to be altered to take a new door frame.
● doors wider than the opening: don't attempt to fit one unless you know how to install a new lintel.
● out-of-square openings: check the lintel, sill and sides carefully with a level, and be prepared to use packing to guarantee a square sub-frame installation so that the doors will run and close correctly.
● the sealed units: when drilling holes in the door frames to add locks, use a hand drill – a power drill could go in too far and touch the edge of the sealed unit, cracking it, which would lead to internal condensation problems between the two panes of glass.

2 Remove the

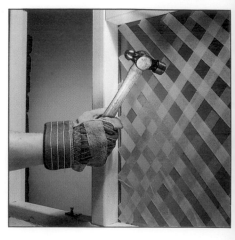

1. Remove hinged windows first, then tape over glass and break carefully with a hammer

To remove the existing door or window frame, whether it's wood or metal, you need to be able to get at the screws or nails holding it in place. Outside, cut back any stucco overlapping the frame neatly using a club hammer and a wide chisel, and rake out any caulking or mortar. On the inside, remove the casing from the old frame and save it to finish off the new doors.

To minimize the risk of littering the site with broken glass, try to unscrew and remove hinged doors and opening windows within the frame. Drill out stubborn screws or punch out the hinge pins to speed up the job. Set these aside, and then tackle areas of fixed glass, covering them with masking tape before breaking the glass with a hammer and lifting out the pieces.

Insert your crowbar between frame and sub-frame and lever to open up the gap as much as possible. Insert a hacksaw blade into the gap and slide it up and down until you encounter the screws or ties (wrap one end in a cloth to protect your hands). Then cut through them to free the frame.

★ TIP

If a hacksaw won't sever the fastenings, insert a slim cold chisel and cut through them – or pull them free – with a sharp blow from the club hammer on the end.

old frame | ### 3 Cut opening | ### 4 Fit sub-frame

2. Pry out the frame slightly with a crowbar then use a hacksaw blade to cut through the fastenings

Rent an angle grinder if you have to cut through a lot of masonry, it saves time and effort

1. Assemble the joints with waterproof woodworking adhesive and leave to dry

Loosen the frame still further by driving your crowbar in underneath the sill. Then use your club hammer and a block of wood to tap it out from inside, working down one side and then the other alternately. Lift it out as a complete unit.

With metal-framed French doors, the door section is usually separate. Drill out any screws, then use a hammer and wood block to knock the door frame inwards, breaking the bond of the putty in which it is bedded. Tackle the side windows in the same way, then remove the main metal frame, followed by the wooden sub-frame to expose the rough opening.

⭐ **TIP**

With wooden frames, don't waste time trying to remove the frame in one piece unless it comes out easily. Saw through each frame member at an angle, then simply pry the sections of the frame out one by one.

Finally, remove the remains of the old screws or ties left round the opening, and chop out any wooden plugs you find – they won't be re-used, and might be rotten as well.

Tidy up the edges of the opening on the inside and outside to provide as flat a surface as possible for the new wooden sub-frame.

The next stage is to remove any partial walls that flanked the old French doors or stood beneath the old window sill: your doors should be close to this width but no wider (unless you know how to fit a longer loadbearing lintel).

Use a wooden straightedge and a level to mark a cutting line on the surface of the wall below the sides of the existing opening: do this at each side, indoors and out. Next, cut neatly down the line with your wide chisel and club hammer to leave a neat edge in any stucco covering masonry outdoors.

Cut away individual bricks one by one, working from the top of the area to be removed. On cavity walls, cut through half bricks and alter the internal studs to create the proper new opening.

⭐ **TIP**

You'll get a neater cut and quicker results if you use a rented angle grinder to cut through the brickwork. Wear gloves and a face mask and goggles for protection from brick splinters.

Check the opening height and width; if necessary, remove one or more courses of brickwork beneath the opening. If it is a little too wide, extra packing out may be needed when the frame is installed.

This stage is the most important of the whole installation, since an out-of-square frame will prevent the doors from operating smoothly and make it impossible to get a weatherproof fit for the sliding and fixed panels.

It is possible with some makes of door to fit the metal door frame directly to the house wall, omitting the sub-frame completely. This method can be a useful way round the size problem, enabling a standard door to be installed in a non-standard opening with the minimum of alteration to the masonry at each side.

Lay out the frame components on your patio or lawn (over polyethylene sheeting if the ground is damp) and assemble the components dry. Check the fit of the corner joints and double-check the dimensions, then assemble with waterproof woodworking adhesive and screws.

2. Tack strips of wood across the corners to keep them square and bed the frame on a layer of mortar in a masonry wall

3. Thread a length of plastic plug onto the end of the screw so you can pass both through the frame straight into the masonry

1. Bed the sill section onto the wooden sub-frame with a thick layer of caulking. Screw down tightly and seal the screws with more caulking

★ TIP

Tack 1 × 2 at a 45° angle **across** each corner of the frame. This not only helps to hold the corner joints while the adhesive sets: it also prevents them being strained as you move the frame into place.

On masonry walls apply a thin mortar bed on top of the vapor barrier and carry the frame to the opening. Rest the sill on the mortar bedding and raise the frame into position, checking as you do that the drip channel on the underside of the sill is clear of the masonry beneath. Tap in small wooden wedges near the top corners of the frame to hold it in position while you check that it is truly vertical (not leaning in or out relative to the wall) and that it remains perfectly square.

Don't rely on a small try-square. Either check that the diagonals are exactly equal, or use the method shown in the drawing on p. 49.

If the frame is out of square, drive in wedges between frame and wall at opposite corners to correct the distortion. Don't use them more than about 12in from the corner or you risk bowing the frame members, and this will prevent the door frame from fitting. When the

frame is square, you can insert packing pieces at the screw positions – again, to prevent distortion as the screws are tightened.

If there is a large gap left above the frame, either lay a thicker mortar bed beneath the sill in a masonry wall (up to a maximum of about 1in thick) or use packing pieces tapped in beneath the sill to raise it slightly.

Now mark and drill the holes in the frame to take the screws. They should go into the center of a brick, not into the mortar course. Drill the clearance holes in the frame at the recommended spacing (usually four per side is sufficient) and mark the masonry or studs through each hole. Lift out the frame, drill and plug the holes and re-position the frame. Check that it is square and drive in the screws, making sure their heads are countersunk neatly into the wood.

★ TIP

If the walls at each side of the opening are breeze block or soft brick, use special frame fixings to save having to remove the frame.

Lastly, check again that the frame is square. If it isn't, slacken off the screws and adjust the wedges.

This stage is a close repeat of the previous one, and if that was done carefully and accurately the door frame itself should fit easily and be perfectly square.

Check that the frame is square by measuring the diagonal of the triangle as shown in the drawing. Then remove the brace.

Assemble the frame members using the screws (and sometimes clips) provided. Make sure you have the correct jamb at each side – they are usually cut to match the slope of the sill, and are not interchangeable. The side of the jamb with weather-stripping should generally be towards the inside of the frame opening.

Getting a weatherproof seal between the door frame and the sub-frame is essential. Water penetration will lead to moisture in the walls and rotting in the frame (and in any floor joists next to the sill). Bed the sill section on a generous bed of caulking, wiping off any excess once the frame has been screwed into place, and use caulking inside and out to seal the frame joints before installing it. Screw the frame in place, then seal all the screw holes in the sill section with caulking and pipe a bead of caulking all around the joint between frame and sub-frame.

frame

2. Next fit the side sections and seal. Note, though, that some frames are assembled first and secured in position in one piece.

If you are fitting the frame direct to masonry, use ordinary wall plugs or steel anchors and make sure the frame is not distorted as you do them up; if necessary, use packing pieces between frame and wall.

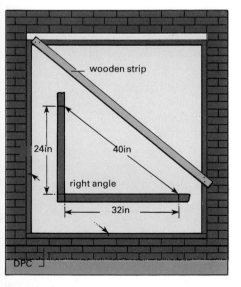

wooden strip

24in

40in

right angle

32in

DPC

To ensure a right angle, measure 24in and 32in along two sides then move the frame until the diagonal measures 40in

6 Installing the doors

Adjust the height of the rollers so the door is exactly square in the frame and fits snugly against it when closed

Follow the individual door manufacturer's instructions carefully for this stage – the precise installation details vary from brand to brand.

Install the fixed pane(s) first, after attaching any brackets needed to the frame with self-tapping screws. You may have to drill these holes yourself, so make sure you have sharp twist drills of the right size ready. Then lift the panel up, slot its top edge into the frame head and swing it down so you can engage the bottom edge on the sill. Slide it along until it's firmly against the frame jamb and attach it to the brackets.

Next, cut and fit the threshold strip between the fixed pane and the lock jamb. Make sure its weatherstripping is in place, and seal screw holes with caulking.

Lift the sliding door into position on the track and move it across to the lock jamb. Adjust the height of the door rollers to ensure that the door closes evenly, by inserting a screwdriver into a hole near the bottom of the door's stile.

★ TIP

Get your helper to take the weight off the rollers as you adjust them by inserting a lever between the door and the sill and lifting up the door. This makes it easier to adjust the screw.

Attach the lock striking plate to the frame jamb, leaving the screws loose so its position can be adjusted to align with the door lock. Attach the door lock, then close the door almost fully so you can adjust the position of the lock striking plate. Add the outside pull handle.

Finally, add any other accessories your door includes – rubber door buffers against which the door opens, anti-lift devices to stop the doors being lifted off their tracks, and additional security locks.

Finish off the installation by putting the trim back around the subframe indoors and out, treating any unfinished wood with preservative, varnish or paint as appropriate. Then seal the join between the subframe and the exterior finish with a further bead of caulking.

Anti-lift devices are essential for patio doors as without them a burglar could lift up the door and swing it out off its track as easily as you installed it in the first place.

The solution is to put some sort of hardware into the gap between the top of the door and the inside of the frame, while still allowing the door to slide freely.

Special anti-lift devices are available. These are small blocks which you screw to the top of the frame inside the channel. But a simple answer – and one approved of by the police – is to slide a length of wood onto the top of the door once the door is in place. Since the sliding door is almost always on the interior, the piece of wood cannot be removed from outside.

A security lock should also be added and, in fact, this is often supplied with the kit. Screw this to the door jamb of the sliding section, near the bottom of the door. When the door is closed the lock can be operated to send a bolt into the frame of the fixed panel, locking the two panels together. You can also use this to lock the door partially open leaving a small gap for ventilation.

Brick Barbecue

Eating outside is one of the joys of the summer months, and a barbecue is equally useful for a party or a quiet evening for two. This easy-to-build barbecue can be adapted in size and shape to suit your yard and cooking requirements perfectly.

It's easy to go out and buy a ready-made barbecue, but much more satisfying to build a permanent version of your own. For a start, it will be a unique creation around which you'll be proud to entertain your friends. Better still, you'll be able to tailor-make it to suit your own back yard.

There's no complicated bricklaying involved in building this simple design, and it's easy to alter the size and shape if you want to. All

you need to be able to do is lay a level base.

One point needs thinking about: the siting of the barbecue. Do you want it in the sun or shade (remember the different directions of the sun throughout the day)? Do you want it near the house or as far away as possible? Will it be part of an existing patio and what about wind directions that could cause smoke and smells to annoy you or your neighbors?

CHECKLIST

Tools
trowel and string line
club hammer and wide cold chisel
level and straightedge
electric drill
screwdriver
shovel

Materials
grills and metal trays
¼sq yd sand; cement
mixed aggregate
metal supports
metal strip 20in long
wood for table and door
door hinges and latch

See Skills Guide pp.
123–126, 130–134 and 138

BARBECUE DESIGN

The basic barbecue consists of two chambers, one housing the grill itself and the other acting as covered storage for charcoal, plates, cutlery and so on.

It's seven and a half bricks wide by two and a half bricks deep, and the dividing wall is bonded to the rear wall. The table is set down two courses to shelter food.

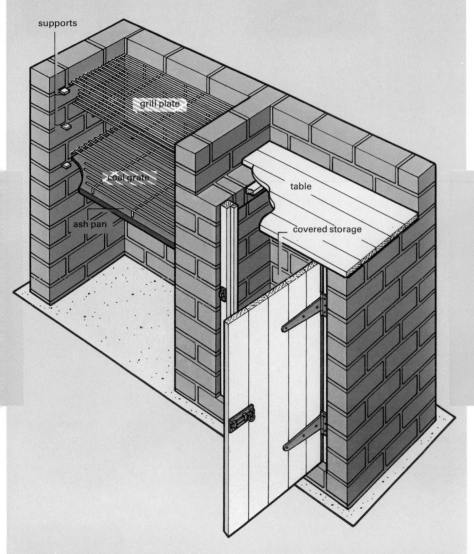

supports
grill plate
coal grate
ash pan
table
covered storage

There are several simple variations you can make to the design above. For a large cooking area you could build two grill chambers side by side. The cupboard could be made longer, perhaps with double doors, giving lots of extra storage space as well as a longer table. The table could be made from exterior plywood, stained and varnished, as could the door. And you could use decorative stone instead of brick. The internal dimensions of the barbecue chamber must be kept constant to match the grill and pan size.

The three support levels give several cooking options. For normal cooking put the fire on the lowest level and the grill in the middle. Move the grill up for slow cooking, and move both up a level if there is little wind.

LAY THE FOUNDATIONS

The foundations consist of a slab of concrete cast in situ over a bed of gravel and held in place by wooden formwork.

The walls of the barbecue will be twelve courses high, so the end wall will measure about 32in high by 21in wide. The base is 3in wider all round

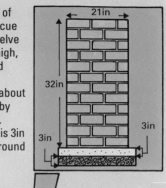

21in
32in
3in
3in

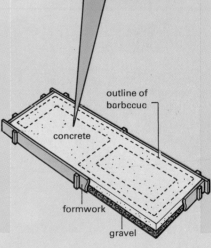

outline of barbecue
concrete
formwork
gravel

Dry lay the first course of bricks to work out the best position for the barbecue then mark the area for the foundations.

Dig down 6in, checking the site is level. Place formwork around the edge if the soil is crumbly and lay down a 3in layer of gravel. Pour on a concrete mix of 1:3:4 (cement: sand: coarse aggregate) and smooth it flat with a shovel or trowel.

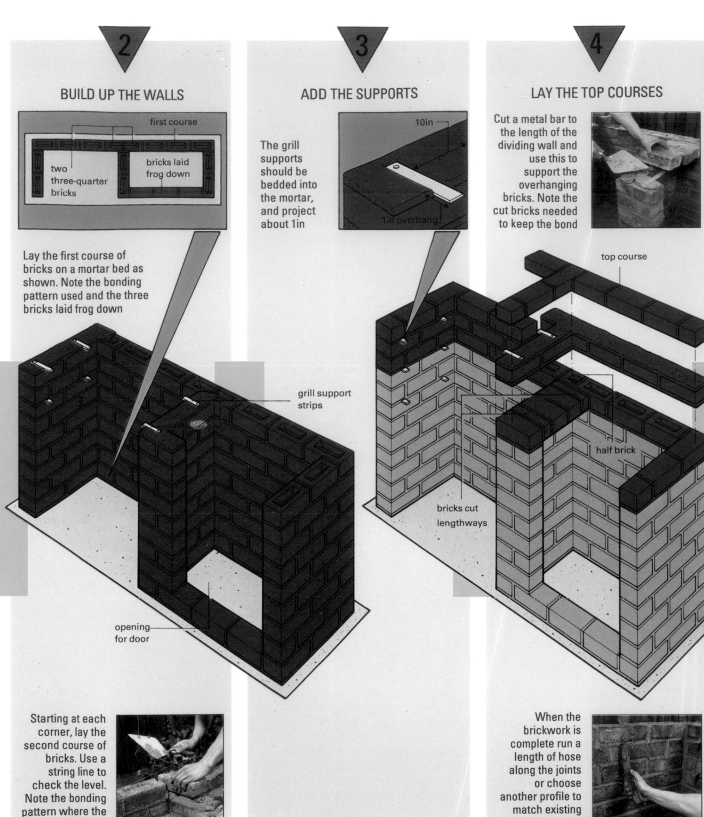

▼2 BUILD UP THE WALLS

first course

two three-quarter bricks

bricks laid frog down

Lay the first course of bricks on a mortar bed as shown. Note the bonding pattern used and the three bricks laid frog down

grill support strips

opening for door

Starting at each corner, lay the second course of bricks. Use a string line to check the level. Note the bonding pattern where the walls meet

Build up the walls in running bond, alternating the two bonding patterns and cutting bricks where necessary. Continue up the seven courses.

▼3 ADD THE SUPPORTS

The grill supports should be bedded into the mortar, and project about 1in

10in

1in overhang

Bed the grill supports into the mortar so they are about 10in apart. The first set should be located between the seventh and eighth courses.

▼4 LAY THE TOP COURSES

Cut a metal bar to the length of the dividing wall and use this to support the overhanging bricks. Note the cut bricks needed to keep the bond

top course

half brick

bricks cut lengthways

When the brickwork is complete run a length of hose along the joints or choose another profile to match existing brickwork

Complete the main structure by adding the last few courses. Remember to lay the overhanging bricks and the top course frog side down.

MAKE THE TABLE AND DOOR

Cut the softwood to length and glue the sections together using waterproof adhesive, holding them in place with bar clamps until dry

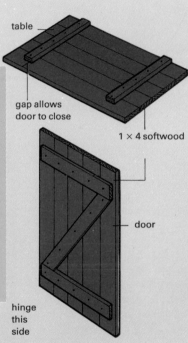

table

gap allows door to close

1 × 4 softwood

door

hinge this side

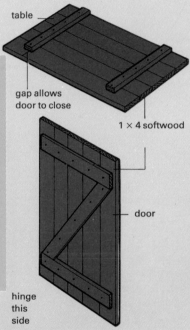

For strength, screw wooden strips to the back of the table and door. On the table cut these back to allow the door to close; on the door make a Z shape

Measure the areas for the table and door, cut the wood to size and glue and screw together. Treat with preservative, and paint or varnish to finish off.

COMPLETE THE BARBECUE

Slide the ash pan and coal grate onto the lower supports and the grill onto the center supports. The top ones are mostly used for slow cooking

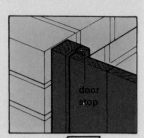

Use 2 × 2 strips for the main door frame and then nail on a 1 × 1 door stop

door stop

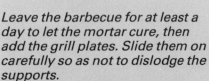

framework screwed to sides

door catch

When the mortar has thoroughly set, drill and plug the walls to take the door frame, then hang the door. Use rust proof hinges and screws

The strap hinges are screwed onto the door and frame — there is no need to recess them

strap hinge

Leave the barbecue for at least a day to let the mortar cure, then add the grill plates. Slide them on carefully so as not to dislodge the supports.

When you've hung the door lay the table in place and pipe a bead of caulking round the edge to seal it to the bricks and prevent water seeping into the cupboard.

CHECKLIST

Tools
try square and marking tools
steel tape measure
jigsaw or saber saw
backsaw
chisels
electric drill and bits
dowel jig (optional)
C clamps
furniture clamps
sewing equipment for making
    cushions

Materials
2 × 4, 1 × 4, 2 × 2, 1 × 2 finished
    softwood
¼in and ½in softwood dowel
¾in plywood scraps
½in steel tubing
washers and cotter pins
No. 10 woodscrews
foam padding and covering
    material

Reclining Sunbed

If sitting on the ground to catch the sun doesn't appeal this cheap and simple sunbed design is the perfect answer.

Reclining wooden sunbeds are quite often seen lined up at fashionable beach hotels, at home you're more likely to see sunbeds and recliners made from synthetic webbing, or stretchy, hammock-like panels, strung across plastic coated or galvanized steel tube frames.
The trouble is that, whatever method is used to protect the metal,

after a few years of being stored in damp conditions – such as garages or sheds, which are often the only space available – corrosion will start breaking through.
Not so with a properly painted or stained wooden sunbed. The only metal parts on this are the galvanized steel tube axle and the treated screws and washers which the backrest pivots around.
The backrest has an adustable recline facility which you can set wherever you want – it's just a matter of forming slots in the tops of the side members. It also folds flat

for easier storage when the sunbed is not in use. Wheels allow you to transport the sunbed easily, unlike some types of recliner which have to be carried – awkward if they cannot be folded.
You should find construction of the sunbed both easy and cheap – the bridle joints which hold the legs to the side members are little more complicated than halving joints, but if you take your time and measure accurately they shouldn't cause you any trouble.
See Skills Guide pp. 112, 114, 116, 117, 119, 121 and 122.

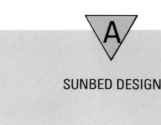

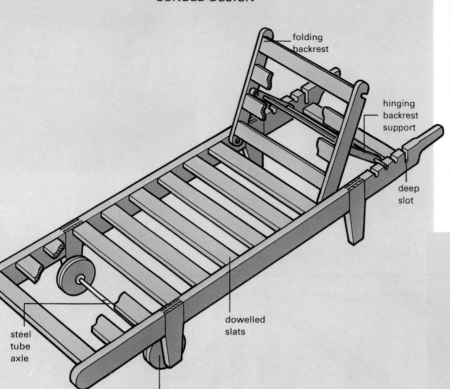

folding
backrest

hinging
backrest
support

deep
slot

dowelled
slats

steel
tube
axle

plywood
wheels

Glue two
scraps of
plywood
together to
give the
thickness for
the wheels.
Clamp
together until
glue is dry

¾in plywood

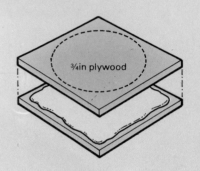

When the glue has completely dried, clamp
down the plywood and cut out wheel

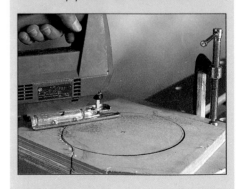

The sunbed is constructed mainly from 2 × 4 finished softwood, although the support slats are only 1 × 4 and the backrest supports are of a much smaller section. The backrest itself is made up in much the same way as the main frame is constructed, but its side members are of 1 × 3 finished softwood instead. It also has to be narrower than the main unit so it can fit between the two side frames. The backrest is supported in the raised position by a small frame with a cross-dowel at the bottom; the cross-dowel is held in place by shallow slots cut in the top of the side members. Cut a deep slot in the side frames behind the backrest support slots to house the cross-dowel so that the backrest will lie flush when folded.

The only difficult part of the job is making the bridle joints, but these are only like double-sided halving joints. To ensure accuracy, once you've set the marking gauge to exactly one third of the width of the wood mark all the joints on sides and legs at one time. Remove the waste wood from the leg first as this is the trickiest part – if you get it slightly wrong, all you have to do is adjust the cutouts on the side members accordingly, so it's important to check the leg against the side before completing the joint.

The cushions are just pieces of plastic foam cut to the right size and protected by simple loose covers held shut by Velcro fasteners – the cushions are held to the sunbed by cotton ties.

Cut the wheels from scraps of plywood glued together – two ¾in thicknesses will be enough. Mark the circumference of the wheel using compasses and drill the hole in the center.

CUT LEG JOINTS

Mark cutouts for joints and cut down sides. Chisel out waste wood – keep fingers away from blade

FORM HANDLES, ASSEMBLE MAIN BED

Cut out handle shapes on end of sides with a jigsaw. Carry out final shaping and smoothing with Surform and sandpaper

Tape over the area to be drilled to stop the bit slipping. Center punch first.

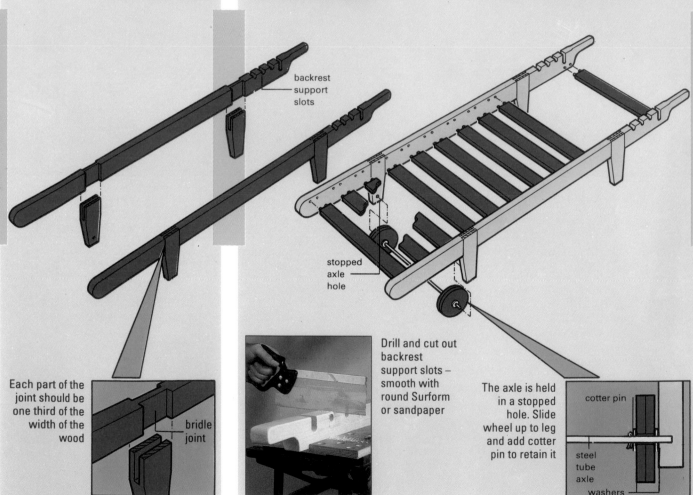

backrest support slots

stopped axle hole

Each part of the joint should be one third of the width of the wood

bridle joint

Drill and cut out backrest support slots – smooth with round Surform or sandpaper

The axle is held in a stopped hole. Slide wheel up to leg and add cotter pin to retain it

cotter pin

steel tube axle

washers

Mark out the legs and side members at the same time with the same gauge, but don't cut wood from the sides until you have the completed legs to check them against.

With the joints made on the side members, shape the handles and cut out the support slot for the backrest. Mark and drill all the dowel holes, ready for main unit assembly.

Cut and drill the axle and fit the sunbed sides together. Where the cotter pin holes go depends on the depth of the stopped hole and the thickness of the wheel and washers: include clearance.

4

MAKE AND ADD BACKREST

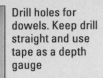

Drill holes for dowels. Keep drill straight and use tape as a depth gauge

Make sure that the backrest screws have adequate clearance

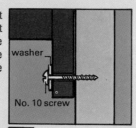

washer

No. 10 screw

5

CUT AND COVER CUSHIONS

Position ties underneath the cushion so that they are concealed when cushion is in place

foam cushion

Velcro fastening

removeable cover

cushion ties

Dry-assemble backrest to check for fit and make adjustments. Reassemble with glue. Clamp square when dry

With the backrest complete, screw it to the sunbed sides. Add backrest support

Make the backrest to fit inside the main frame sides. Use first slat to get the length of all others, then mark and drill dowel holes. Transfer marks to backrest sides, drill holes and assemble.

Drill clearance holes for the screws backrest pivots around. Position backrest, mark through holes, drill pilot holes and screw into place. Make support to suit distance from backrest to slot.

Cut the cushion from a piece of foam – cut it to final size with a large pair of scissors or a sharp utility knife; if you use the knife, lay a sheet of hardboard or cardboard underneath the work to protect your work surface.

Make up the loose covers to fit the cushions by forming a 'bag' inside out, then turn it the right way out to hide the stitching. Use Velcro strips at the open end so that you'll be able to remove the covers easily for washing. Add ties to keep the cushion in place when it is laid in position.

Fold the foam in half to make insertion easier.

CHECKLIST

Tools
pencil and marking tools
handsaw, jigsaw or saber saw
circular saw or router
hammer and screwdrivers
carborundum stone

Materials
sand and white cement
steel reinforcing rod
wood and nails for formwork
release agent
sundial and screws

See Skills Guide
pp. 123 and 131

Sundial

Every garden needs a centerpiece — and a sundial or birdbath is one of the most attractive and entertaining features you can have. A sundial is classic and interesting, while a birdbath and feeding table can provide amusement at all times of the year.

Sundials and birdbaths can be bought at garden centers, but it is much more creative and satisfying to cast your own from concrete. And the techniques used in making these items can be adapted to make other garden items, such as seats.

The material used to make this sundial is white cement, together with white sand — fine sand as used in playgrounds — and coarse sand to provide bulk. This produces a stone-like finish with a very natural appearance. But you may prefer to paint the finished item with exterior masonry paint which will both enhance the appearance and give added protection against the weather.

The design consists of a base, a pillar and a top, which are joined by a steel bar running through the middle of the structure. This also serves to reinforce the sundial pillar. While professionally made ornaments often have curved pillars or involve complicated shapes, it's possible to achieve a very satisfactory effect using easily made wooden formwork, giving straight sides. You can, if you wish, put a great deal of ingenuity into decorating the formwork — by gluing moldings to the inside, to produce a fluted effect along the pillar, for example. But bear in mind that the cast concrete may not release from the formwork if there are vertical edges to be pulled away — angle them so that they pull away cleanly.

You can buy cast brass dials from garden centers fairly cheaply, or buy more elaborate engraved dials from specialist suppliers. Making your own dial is possible if you wish to cut and engrave sheet brass yourself for total accuracy — a sundial should ideally be designed for the precise latitude where it is to be used.

Align the dial so that the gnomon (shadow stick) points exactly north. If you have bought one which is not exactly at the same angle to the horizontal as your latitude you can tilt the whole dial to make it correct and increase its accuracy.

Your dial will tell the correct solar time, but not civil time (such as daylight saving time). The only way to allow for daylight saving on a flat dial is to renumber the hours — turning the whole dial won't work. Bear in mind that civil time can be as much as 16 minutes different and that a further error is introduced the farther east or west you are within your time zone.

A ▼

THE SUNDIAL'S DESIGN

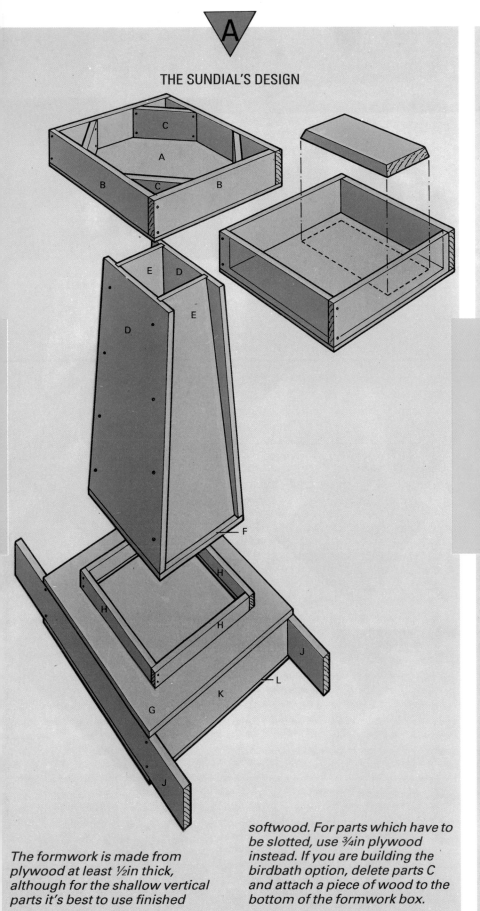

The formwork is made from plywood at least ½in thick, although for the shallow vertical parts it's best to use finished softwood. For parts which have to be slotted, use ¾in plywood instead. If you are building the birdbath option, delete parts C and attach a piece of wood to the bottom of the formwork box.

1 ▼

CUT THE COMPONENTS

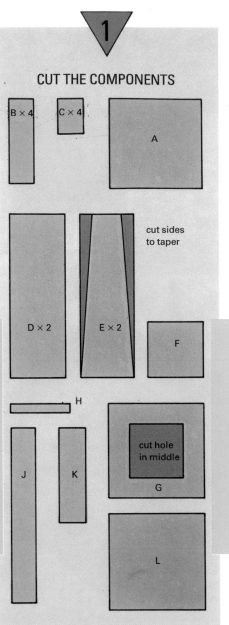

B × 4   C × 4   A

cut sides to taper

D × 2   E × 2   F

H

J   K   G cut hole in middle

L

Mark the tapers – remember to mark the slot on the 'outside' of the mold line

Mark and cut the formwork parts to suit the chosen size and design – avoid deep indentations or acutely concave shapes, as these will make it hard to remove the formwork.

BUILD UP THE FORMWORK AND CAST THE CONCRETE

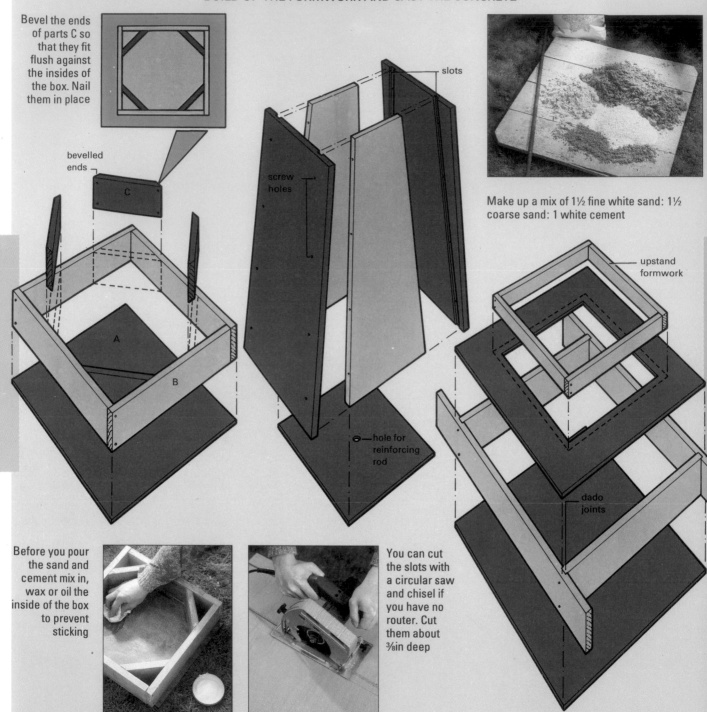

Bevel the ends of parts C so that they fit flush against the insides of the box. Nail them in place

bevelled ends

C

screw holes

A

B

slots

hole for reinforcing rod

Make up a mix of 1½ fine white sand: 1½ coarse sand: 1 white cement

upstand formwork

dado joints

Before you pour the sand and cement mix in, wax or oil the inside of the box to prevent sticking

You can cut the slots with a circular saw and chisel if you have no router. Cut them about ⅜in deep

Build up the formwork sides on the plywood base. Make sure that the surface of the plywood is blemish-free as this will be molding the top face of the structure, cast upside-down.

Aim to make the sides a tight fit in their slots to stop the sand and cement leaking out: it doesn't matter if you have to tap the parts together. Don't forget the hole in the base for the reinforcing rod.

Pour the concrete mix into the molds, using a stick to tamp it well into the corners — especially under the upstand on the base. Tap the molds to release any trapped pockets of air.

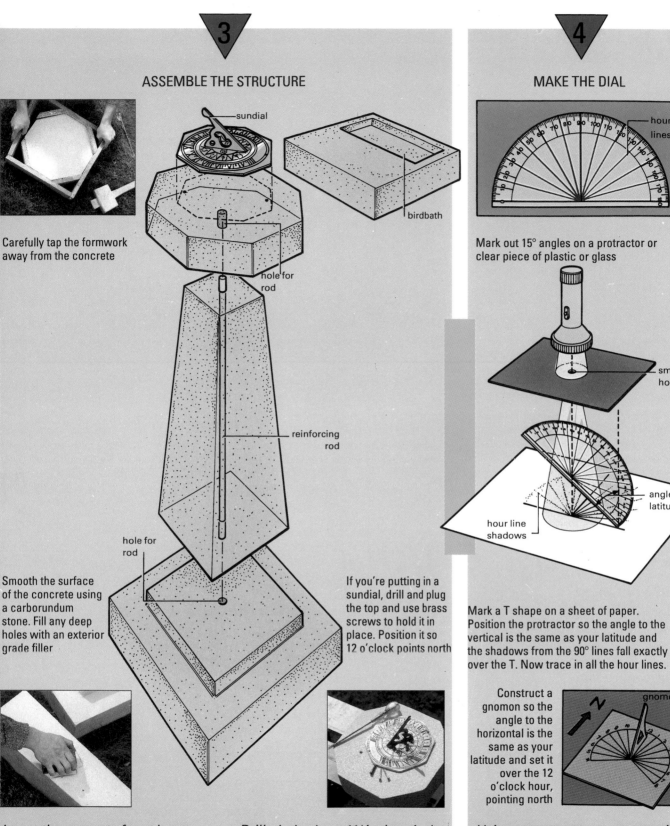

3 ASSEMBLE THE STRUCTURE

sundial

birdbath

hole for rod

reinforcing rod

hole for rod

Carefully tap the formwork away from the concrete

Smooth the surface of the concrete using a carborundum stone. Fill any deep holes with an exterior grade filler

If you're putting in a sundial, drill and plug the top and use brass screws to hold it in place. Position it so 12 o'clock points north

Leave the concrete for at least a day to set then carefully remove all the formwork. Smooth the surface to remove any marks left by the mold and round off the edges slightly. Paint if required.

Drill a hole about 1¼in deep in the center of the base and in the underside of the top section, wide enough to take the ends of the reinforcing rod. Then assemble the whole structure.

4 MAKE THE DIAL

hour lines

small hole

angle of latitude

hour line shadows

Mark out 15° angles on a protractor or clear piece of plastic or glass

Mark a T shape on a sheet of paper. Position the protractor so the angle to the vertical is the same as your latitude and the shadows from the 90° lines fall exactly over the T. Now trace in all the hour lines.

gnomon

Construct a gnomon so the angle to the horizontal is the same as your latitude and set it over the 12 o'clock hour, pointing north

Using a protractor you can easily make your own sundial to suit your exact latitude (your latitude will be shown on a map). The hour lines can be engraved on brass or carved into the concrete.

Tools
backsaw, rip saw
1in chisel
sledge hammer
tape measure, ruler
level
electric drill and ¼in bit
wrench
pencil
step ladder

Materials
rough cut wood
4 × 7ft 6in lengths of 4 × 4
2 × 8ft of 2 × 6
7 × 10ft of 2 × 6
8 × ⅜in galvanized lag bolts
4 steel fence post supports
wood preservative

Options
brass hooks, wooden trellis

See Skills Guide
pp. 116, 122 and 137

Build a Pergola

Build this wooden pergola and create a cool and shady spot under which to relax on hot summer days. The simple design can be easily adapted to suit any garden or patio and is ideal for clematis, roses and other climbing plants.

A garden or patio without the shade of trees or buildings can often become too hot to sit in comfortably in the height of summer. A pergola with carefully trained plants and creepers provides not only welcome shade but makes an attractive garden feature.

The pergola design is extremely versatile and can be altered to almost any size, but do make sure that it is tall enough for you and your family to walk under without any trouble.

If you reduce the size of the pergola to a great extent, choose wood of smaller dimensions to keep the design in proportion. A simple rose arbour can be made with 2 × 2 uprights and a framework of 2 × 3. Likewise, a covered walkway sheltering a garden path can be built.

Built next to the house, the pergola frame makes a good alternative car port with a concrete, flagstone or gravel base. Add plastic corrugated sheets to the frame for a weather-proof covering.

There are many attractive flowering plants that you can train to grow over your pergola. The rose is probably the most popular. Although they may take many years to mature the result is usually spectacular

and very rewarding. It is worth adding a wooden garden trellis to the pergola posts to help train your roses. Choose varieties with the prefix 'climbing' such as 'Climbing Iceberg' and 'Climbing Masquerade'. Ask at your local garden center about varieties which have been bred to flower throughout the season. Another attractive shrub is Wistaria sinensis, a deciduous climber with drooping racemes of mauve flowers which bloom in early summer. For color in the winter, choose an evergreen climber which provides foliage all year round – your local garden center can provide you with advice and information.

If you plan to build the pergola close to your house, bear in mind that any plants or creepers that you grow will obscure the light from nearby windows. Once established, shrubs need good regular pruning to train them over the pergola.

THE PERGOLA DESIGN

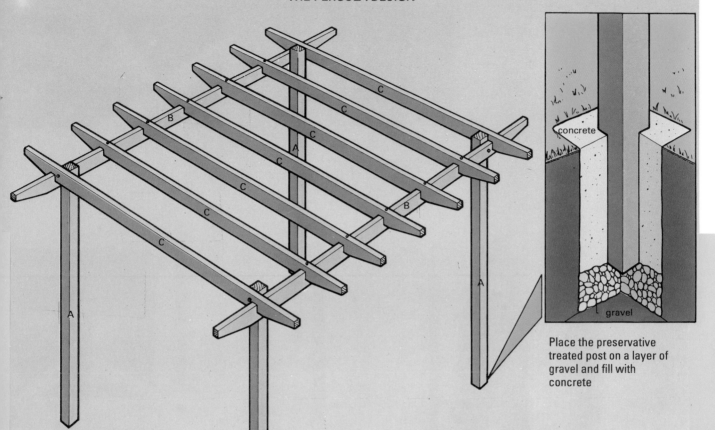

Place the preservative treated post on a layer of gravel and fill with concrete

The frame of the pergola is constructed from lengths of rough sawn lumber — four upright posts made from 4 × 4 softwood, and a framework consisting of two supporting bars and seven cross pieces made from 2 × 6 softwood. The uprights can be supported by steel fence posts which make the erection quick and easy and also protect the posts from rotting below ground level.

Halving joints enable the cross pieces to slot neatly on to the front and back supporting bars. It is best to mark the position of the joints while the framework is on the ground — this will ensure a perfect fit as rough sawn lumber is not always accurately cut.

⅜in lag bolts secure the framework to the uprights and hold each halving joint together.

Check the uprights with a level before attaching the two supporting bars, and check that the supporting bars are level before inserting the lag bolts.

An alternative to erecting the pergola with steel fence posts is to sink the uprights into concrete.

In this case you will have to add at least 16in extra to the length of the four uprights and soak the ends which are to be buried overnight in a bucket of wood preservative. Mark a line around the post at ground level as a positioning guide. Dig a vertical hole at least 30in deep using a spade or a rented post hole borer and fill the bottom with gravel. Sink the post into the ground and add two wooden braces. Check that it is vertical with a level. Pack gravel around the post and shovel in concrete. Trowel the surface to a slope so any water runs away from the post.

1
CUT THE COMPONENTS

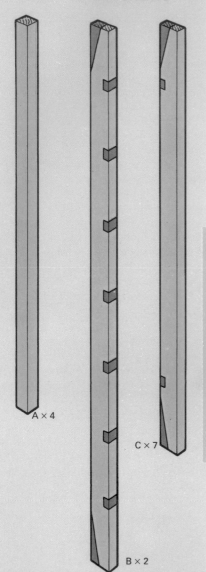

A × 4

C × 7

B × 2

Mark a line 2in up and 10in along from the bottom corner of parts B and C. Use a rip saw

Buy the wood cut to length from your local lumberyard or supplier. If you are setting the posts into concrete, remember to add at least 16in to the length of each upright. Cut the overhang sections on parts B and C.

2
ERECT THE POSTS

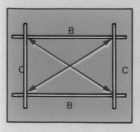

Lay framework on the ground in position. Diagonal measurements must be equal for the frame to be 'square'

Check the 12in overhang on B and C, then mark the halving joint position

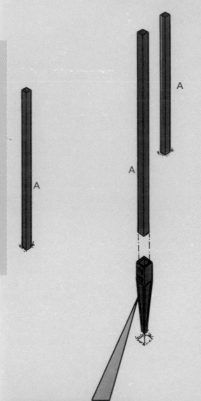

Tap the fence posts in each corner of the frame to mark position accurately

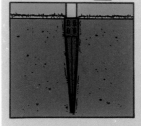

Drive the fence posts in the center of the marked position using a mallet and a piece of scrap wood to protect the top of the posts

Set up the framework on the ground and then mark each halving joint individually to ensure a perfect fit

Lay the outer frame on the ground in position. Check that it is 'square' using the method shown above. Mark the position of the halving joints where C crosses B. Use an inverted fence post to mark the position of the posts.

Place the rest of the cross pieces at regular intervals along parts B and mark their position. Remove the framework and drive in posts.

3

SECURE THE SUPPORTING BARS

Use lag bolts to secure parts B and C to upright post A. End part C should be level with the top of the upright posts

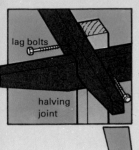

lag bolts

halving joint

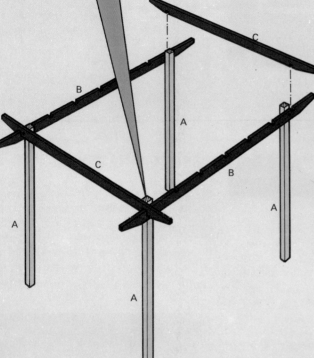

C

B

A

C

B

A

A

A

A

4

ADD THE CROSS PIECES

Drill pilot holes through each halving joint and drive lag bolts with a wrench

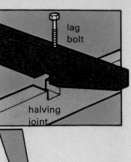

lag bolt

halving joint

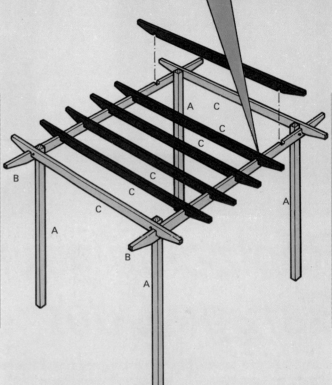

A

C

C

C

C

C

C

C

B

A

A

A

B

A

Cut the halving joints with a backsaw. Chisel out debris

Use a wrench to tighten the lag bolts

Drive the four uprights into the metal fence posts with a sledgehammer. Cut the halving joints 1in deep in parts B and 1½in deep in parts C. Position parts B on the upright posts and drill screw holes.

Drill the pilot hole for lag bolts using a ¼in bit

Screw in brass hooks to the overhang for hanging baskets

Drive lag bolts into each halving joint to secure parts B and C together. Finish with a colored wood preservative. Attach brass hooks to the overhangs for hanging baskets.

65

■ PROJECT

Replacing your Garage Door

Overhead garage doors are everyone's first choice for most typical one- and two-car garages nowadays. They're easy to install, light to operate and simple to maintain – a far cry from old-fashioned hinged wooden doors – and come in a range of styles and sizes to suit almost every existing garage. You can open them automatically by installing the appropriate gear and controls.

Garage doors of this type work exactly as their name implies – by travelling upwards and overhead as they are opened, coming to rest in a horizontal position underneath the garage roof. Two different mechanisms are used to raise the doors. Either the top corners of the door slide backwards along tracks positioned within the garage, or the whole door swings on two spring-loaded or counterbalanced pivot arms. The former, known as tracked doors, usually retract fully into the garage when they are opened, while the latter, known as trackless or

canopy doors, project by about a third of their height from the front of the garage when open.

Tracked types are generally a little more involved to install and obviously take up more space within the garage; trackless versions are simpler to install and the projecting canopy may be a useful feature if you want to work on your car under cover. Tracked canopy types offer a compromise – short tracks within the garage leaving a projecting canopy when open and taking up less space within the roof area of the garage itself.

① What the job involves

Choosing and installing a new overhead garage door is generally a straightforward job, but certainly requires two pairs of hands. There are six main stages.
● Choose the style of door you want for your garage – ribbed, panelled, with glazed sections and so on.
● Measure the existing door opening accurately.
● Find a firm making doors in the style and size you want, and place your order.
● Remove the existing doors.
● Repair or replace the existing frame as necessary.
● Install the door and its associated tracks, pivot arms and springs within the door opening.

BEFORE YOU START

● Collect literature from a number of door manufacturers, so you can get a clear idea of what's available in terms of both looks and sizes. Steel and aluminum types are the most common (and the cheapest); fiberglass types generally cost more, while

CHECKLIST

Tools
steel tape measure
electric drill
twist and masonry drills
screwdrivers
wrenches
hacksaw
chisel and mallet
level

Materials
garage door
new sub-frame (if required)
screws and wallplugs
caulking
paint
lubricating oil

 See Skills Guide
p. 138

wooden doors work out most expensive of all.

● Decide on which type of opening mechanism you prefer. Tracked types require attachment to either the garage walls or the roof structure and generally fit within an existing (or new) wooden door frame; trackless types are put up within the door opening itself, either direct to the masonry or to a wooden sub-frame. Fully retracting tracked types obviously limit storage beneath the garage roof – worth thinking about if you use this area for storing your building materials.

● Measure accurately, following the instructions given by the maker of the door you have selected. Some firms ask for measurements to be taken within the existing wooden frame, others prefer masonry-to-masonry figures where appropriate. Check your measurements carefully to the nearest $\frac{1}{16}$in.

The two main types of overhead doors are the canopy door (left) and the tracked door (right). Both are easy to install and come in kit form with all the necessary hardware

● Place your order and confirm the delivery date, so you can plan the job for a specific time
● Read the installation instructions carefully so you are clear about the procedure and can identify every part before you start work.

! WATCH OUT FOR

● Non-standard door openings. The doors will be more expensive than standard sizes, and it may be easier and more economical to alter the size of the opening by putting in a new wooden sub-frame first.
● Obstructions within the garage. Check the clearances required by the manufacturer below the garage roof and at each side, where lever arms may need room to operate.
● Decay in the existing door frame. This will need repairing before the new door is put up and if it's serious a completely new frame may be required.
● Hidden extras in the price list. Make sure that the prices quoted include sales tax and delivery, and check the extra cost of accessories such as locks, handles and so on.

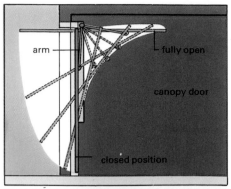

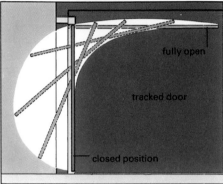

The canopy door projects from the garage when open while the tracked door retracts fully to the inside of the garage

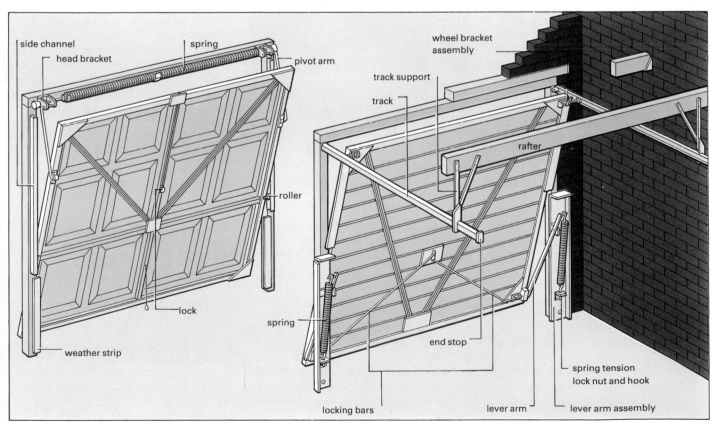

2 Prepare the opening

Once your new door has arrived and you have all the tools and materials you need, start by removing the old garage door.

If you have hinged doors, prop them open and try to undo the screws holding the hinges to the frame. These will probably be rusty and encrusted with paint; try not to damage the frame as you attempt to remove them.

If the old door is the overhead canopy type first insert the pin in the right-hand end of the spring mechanism to hold the tension in the spring then carefully undo all the bolts and screws. (If you have lost the original locking pin there will be one supplied with the new door. The pin must be put in place because the stored energy in the spring is enough to break a person's arm, if released suddenly.) Have a helper on hand to support the tracks if there are any as you free them, and to take the weight of the door itself.

★ TIP

If the old screws are stuck fast, try heating their heads with a soldering iron – the expansion often loosens the grip of the threads. If this fails, drill off the screw heads. Apply penetrating oil to stubborn nuts.

With the old door(s) removed, check the condition of the door frame if you plan to reuse it for mounting the new door.

Start by checking that the frame is securely attached to the masonry, and add extra fastenings using screws and plugs if it is at all loose.

Look for signs of decay, especially where the side pieces meet the ground, and scarf-joint in new pieces of wood if the decay is not extensive. Fill all old screw or bolt holes with exterior-quality filler or dowel plugs to finish the preparation of the existing frame.

If the old frame is in really poor condition, it's generally better to replace it completely. You may also want to put up a new frame of thicker or thinner wood to accept a particular size of door. Saw through

1. Prop up the old door with wedges and unscrew the hinges. Remove any bolts

2. Saw off any rabbet in the frame – or pry off a door stop – and finish off the frame

the old frame at intervals, then use a crow-bar to pry it away from the opening. Remove all the old fastenings ready for a new frame to be put in position.

Cut the head and jambs of the new frame to size, and form simple rabbet joints for the top corners. Then apply preservative liberally to the wood before securing each section in place. Check as you drive the screws that the frame stays perfectly square, and insert shims between the frame and the wall if any distortion occurs.

Pipe a bead of caulking all around the frame where it meets the wall to prevent water penetration between the joint.

3 Install the

With the frame prepared or replaced, the door itself can be installed in the opening. How this is tackled will vary from door to door, so it's vital to follow the manufacturer's installation instructions.

Begin by unpacking all the parts supplied, and check that everything is present and can be identified. In particular, make sure you have all the necessary screws if they are not part of the kit.

When you are ready to start work, call your assistant; the first part of the job – positioning the door within the opening – is far easier to do with two pairs of hands. Lift it up and wedge it in position so there is equal clearance all round the frame and beneath the door bottom.

From here onwards, the assembly sequence depends on which type of door gear is being installed. With trackless canopy-type doors put up within a wooden frame, the first stage is to attach the spring operating mechanism to the inner face of the frame head, using screws or bolts through the frame. On some doors you may also have to put up the pivot bars – link the upper ends of the bars, which swing the door upwards as it is opened, to the brackets at each end of the spring mechanism, and link the lower ends to the pivot points on the side edges of the door itself, about a quarter of the way down each side.

1. Prop the door centrally in the opening and put in the screws to take the center support bracket

new door

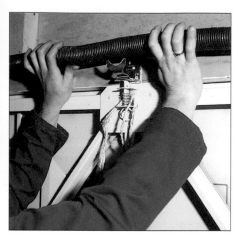

2. *Hook the bracket over the screws and tighten up then lift the spring into place*

3. *Line up the right-hand head bracket so the pivot arms are parallel to the side of the door*

4. *Put up the side channel parallel to the door and with its bottom edge just below the roller*

Next, put up the slim vertical tracks that guide the door to the inner face of the frame, and add the small guide rollers further down the door edges so they locate in the tracks as the door is opened and closed.

★ **TIP**
At this point, check the door operation to see that everything is correctly aligned and works smoothly; then apply a little lubricating oil to the spring and all the pivot points.

Finally, tension the spring mechanism as instructed until the door can be swung open with only the minimum of effort. Then add the weatherstrips to the lower inner face of the frame jambs.

Trackless doors with integral frames are much simpler to install since they usually arrive completely assembled. All you have to do is lift up the complete door-plus-metal-frame assembly to the door opening and screw it in place. You will probably have to make some adjustments to the spring tension once the door is in position.

With **tracked doors,** attach the roller guides to the top edge of the door sides to act as a positional guide for putting up the door tracks. Then screw or bolt the front end of the track to the door frame in line with the roller guides.

★ **TIP**
Leave the fastenings loose at this stage, so you can swing the track up to the required angle and mark the positions for the support brackets at the other end of the track.

Most tracks are set at a slight angle to the horizontal. Some are designed for suspension from the garage ceiling via metal straps, while others are attached to wooden packing blocks attached to the garage wall. With the suspended type, you may have to put up additional supports across the garage roof if the joists are not in the right position for direct attachment. With the straps or blocks in place, swing up and attach the track in its final position. Add a buffer at each inner end.

Next, attach one end of each lever arm to the lower pivot point on the door frame, swing it up to the vertical and mark the position of the spring lever arm assembly on the frame. Secure this in place with screws or bolts as specified, and connect the upper end of the lever arm to it. Put up the springs; then adjust the spring tension so that the door opens easily, and will balance itself roughly half open.

Finish off the door installation by lubricating all the pivot points. Then add the door stops and weather-stripping to the frame.

5. *Holding the side cable taut, carefully pull out the locking pin, then test the operation of the door.*

6. *Add a door stop or weather strip to the lower edges of the door frame on the inside.*

4 Add the lock and finish off

Complete the door installation by adding the handle and lock, and connecting up the cables or long metal locking bars that secure the door within its frame.

Get your assistant to position the external handle while you lift up the internal one into position on its spindle and do up the bolts that hold the two parts of the handle assembly together.

With some doors, the locking bars fit through small staples on the door edges, in line with the central handle, and slide horizontally as the handle is turned. With others, they run downwards toward the bottom corners of the door and are connected there to small bolts already mounted on the door itself. The latter type offers marginally better security against the door being forced open.

★ TIP

With the horizontal bar type, make sure the internal handle is in the 'unlocked' position; then swing the locking bars up to the edge of the door to check that they do not protrude beyond the edge of the weatherstrip. If they do, cut them down slightly with a hacksaw.

Position the end of each locking bar in its staple on the door edge, or connect it to its bolt lower down the door. Then close the door and operate the internal handle to lock it. Check that the locking operation is smooth and positive, and lubricate all the linkages.

Most steel and aluminum doors are sold either with a factory-applied finish (available in an increasing range of colors) or just primed ready for you to paint in the color of your choice.

To paint the door, rub down any rough edges with wet-and-dry abrasive paper and touch in scratches with the appropriate metal primer — calcium plumbate on galvanized doors, zinc phosphate on aluminum ones. Then wipe the door with solvent to degrease it, and apply one or two undercoats followed by a top coat of high gloss paint.

1. With the handle locked in the upright position push it into the pre-drilled holes in the door

2. Locate the back plate assembly over the lock spindle and screw to the inside of the door

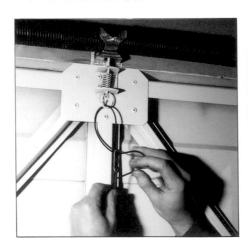

3. Loop the lock cable over the pin on the back plate, attach to the bolt and pull the cord tight

■ Options

Install an automatic door opener. This allows you the luxury of being able to drive into your garage without having to get out and open the doors yourself. The system consists of a motor mounted beneath the garage ceiling and a drive arm attached to the door to pull it open.

The motor can be activated by either infra-red or radio remote control, or by a key inserted in a post-mounted 'lock' in the driveway.

Check that it incorporates an automatic reverse mechanism (this opens the door again immediately if it strikes an obstruction as it is closing) and a manual override facility so it can be opened by hand in the event of a power failure.

Remote control devices use infra-red or radio signals and operate from inside the car

The motor units can be installed to fit most doors and often include a light fixture as well

1 What the job involves

Replacing your rainwater system is a straightforward off-with-the-old, on-with-the-new exercise, involving nothing more difficult than careful measuring and perhaps a little wrestling with old fastenings.
You have to:
● dismantle the old downspouts, working from the bottom upwards
● free the old gutter lengths from their supporting brackets – or from the fascia itself
● remove all the old fastenings from fascias and walls, and repair any defects you come across
● install the new guttering to the correct fall towards the outlets
● add the new downspouts, and make provision for the rainwater run-off to enter a storm drain or drywell.

CHECKLIST

Tools
hacksaw
crowbar
filling knife
tape measure
string line
plumb bob
level
screwdriver(s)
general-purpose saw
electric drill + bits
ladder

Materials
gutter/downspout lengths
corners (inside/outside)
drop outlets
connectors
gutter/downspout brackets and
  hangers
exterior quality filler
primer/paint as required
screws/wallplugs

See Skills Guide p. 139

Putting up New Guttering

If you have an old-fashioned system of gutters and downspouts, the chances are that it doesn't work very well. This is probably due to a combination of neglect and old age, but modern plastic rainwater products offer a system that's easy to install and maintain.

Efficient rainwater disposal is a must for every home. Roofs collect a surprisingly large amount of water whenever it rains, and as it runs off it should be collected by the gutters and channelled via a series of downspouts to ground level, where it will flow either into storm drains or into a drywell in the yard. However, if your gutters and downspouts don't work properly, the result will be rotten eaves and damp walls.

The problem may be caused by a simple blockage, which can easily be cleared. But if the brackets supporting the gutters and downspouts have broken, or rust and physical damage have caused holes and cracks to open up, it will be better in the long run to replace the entire system. Modern plastic rainwater products are light in weight, so they're easy to install, and they require virtually no maintenance once they have been put up. Joints are made with simple clip-together components which are waterproof if properly assembled. The job requires no special tools, and can be carried out in a weekend.

BEFORE YOU START

● Decide which rainwater system you are going to install. Plastic is the obvious choice as it is durable and easy to install, but on a period building you may want to put up new cast iron or aluminum gutters in a traditional style. If you are planning to replace only certain sections of the guttering then you should take a sample of the existing gutter to your local supplier to match up the new sections as closely as possible. Do not connect aluminum gutters to either copper or steel in any combination because of the corrosive effect of the electrolytic action.

● Choose the gutter profile and color you want. Half round squared and ogee are all popular. White, grey and black are offered by most manufacturers; some also do brown, green and cream.

● Pick the correct size for your roof area. For most houses, 4in gutters and 2½in downspouts are adequate, but you may need 6in gutters and 4in downspouts for roofs with a very large surface area. As a general guide, replace existing gutters with new gutters of the same dimension.

● Measure the lengths of the gutter and downspout runs carefully. You can measure the former more easily at ground level but you'll have to climb a ladder to measure the downspout drops. While you're up

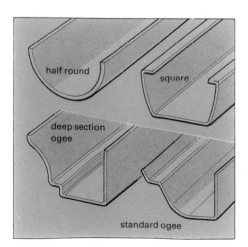

Gutter lengths come in a variety of profiles and colors which vary from one manufacturer to another

To gauge the length of gutters and downspouts count the courses of bricks and the bricks across

there, make a note of the amount by which overhanging eaves project beyond the face of the wall below – an elbow will be needed to join the gutter drop outlet to the downspout.

● work out what pieces will be needed to make up the gutter runs. You will need drop outlets to connect to each downpipe, 90° inside and outside corner pieces and possibly 135° ones too if you have angled bays, connectors and brackets to connect the components and secure them in place. If you have overhanging eaves you'll need 135° elbows to join between the outlets and the top of the downspouts. Plan to have a downspout for every 35ft run of guttering even if that means altering the old existing arrangements. Lastly, think about how the downspout will discharge. Set a splash block under the elbow at the bottom of each downspout to direct the water away from the foundation of the house. Otherwise connect the downspouts to the storm drain or a separate drywell set far away from the house in the middle of the yard.

● Collect together some suitable access equipment. At the very least you'll need an extension ladder. A slot-together platform tower with wheels is a better bet on level sites but you must have a solid surface all around the house for it to stand on. If you're taking down old cast iron guttering, you'll need a helper.

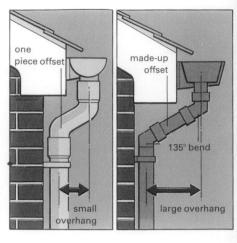

For overhanging eaves, use a double bend or make an offset with two 135° elbows and a short length

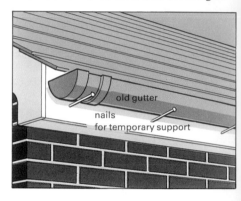

If you do not have help, support the old gutter with nails until you can lift it off its bracket

WATCH OUT FOR

● old guttering that's seriously damaged by rust. It may break away and crash to the ground as you try to dismantle it. Be sure to secure any suspect lengths with rope for extra safety.

● Failed fastenings or rotten fascia boards. Again, the lengths may simply drop if disturbed.

● Dropped slates or tiles resting in the gutter. Lift and reposition any that you find before you start dismantling the gutter itself.

2 Remove the old system

Taking down your existing guttering and downspouts is potentially the most difficult stage of the job, because the old fastenings will have rusted up and may be hard to undo.

Start work at ground level, on the lowest length of the first downspout.

You will probably have a shaped spout or elbow at the bottom of each length, and this will be attached to the wall by nails or screws driven through a strap or bracket around the elbow.

Try to pry out the fastenings with a lever inserted between straps and wall. If this won't free them, either punch them further into the wall or hacksaw through them. Lift off the strap and elbow then set them aside.

Now look up the pipe to the top of the next length. This will also have a supporting strap on its upper end; repeat the process to free it.

⭐ **TIP**

It's a good idea to have a helper to hold the length of old downspout while you tackle the old fastenings, so that it doesn't crash to the ground when you free them.

As you work your way up the length, you may encounter branches connecting other downspout runs to the one you're working on. These are generally a loose fit in the socket end of the length beneath, so be ready to take their weight when the previous pipe length is removed. The same point applies when you reach eaves level; the elbows fit loosely into the previous length.

You can now turn your attention to the guttering itself. Every joint on the run of an old cast iron system will probably be bolted together through the overlapping spigot and socket ends (although you may be lucky enough to find a few loose joints, which were probably leaking anyway). It's generally not worth trying to undo the nuts, since they will probably be completely rusty. Instead, cut through the bolt as close as possible to the underside of each joint, then punch the bolt upwards from below to free the connection. Get your helper to

1. Free the old gutter length from its bracket, carefully lift out and carry down to ground level

steady each length as you free the fastenings. On damaged lighter weight systems simply remove the spikes from the sleeves, or undo the hangers to release the lengths of guttering as you move along.

⭐ **TIP**

If you are working alone, drive 6in nails into the fascia board at about 3ft intervals to support each gutter length until you are able to reposition your ladder and lift the length safely off its brackets.

As you free the fastenings, take down all the small connectors, corners, drop outlets and so on – first. Then lift out the gutter lengths and carry them down to ground level. Don't just drop them; cast iron is brittle, and splinters could injure passers-by or break a ground-floor window. Next, remove all the old gutter brackets from the fascia board. If you find that you have the type of bracket that was nailed to the sides of the rafters rather than being screwed to the fascia, simply cut them off flush with the fascia using a hacksaw. Lift up shingles to remove old hangers.

If you have old ogee gutters attached directly to the fascias, try to lever out the fastenings with a crowbar inserted between gutter and fascia. If this fails, either drill off the

2. Remove brackets from the fascia board, using a claw hammer if necessary

3. If an elbow cannot be easily removed by hand, gently knock it with a hammer

screw heads or use a small cold chisel to cut them off. Again, either have someone to help you or support the weight of the lengths on heavy nails.

⭐ **TIP**

Rather than simply throwing out old iron gutters and downspouts contact a local scrap metal dealer to see what price he will give you for them. There will be quite a weight of metal, and any proceeds can help considerably towards the cost of purchasing the new guttering system.

3 Repairing the fascia boards

With the old gutters and downspouts removed, you're bound to have some repair work to do. Don't skimp on it, or you'll store up future maintenance work unnecessarily.

Examine the condition of the fascia boards carefully. If they're basically sound, fill any splits and old screw or nail holes with exterior quality filler, prime and touch in any bare wood and treat the whole surface with a coat of fresh paint. If the paintwork is peeling and flaking, strip and repaint.

If the fascias are showing signs of decay, you can either patch in new wood or replace them completely.

★ **TIP**

As an alternative to wood for the new fascias, consider vinyl. This type of fascia board can be cut and attached just like ordinary wood, but won't rot and needs no maintenance in the future.

You'll probably find that the downspouts were secured with large nails, either driven direct into the masonry or, more likely, into wooden plugs set in the mortar courses. Pull these plugs out and repair the holes with exterior filler or mortar.

1. Fill holes and splits in the fascia board. Then strip peeling paintwork and repaint

4 Fit the new gutters

1. Hang a plumbline from fascia to splash block to determine the position of the gutter drop outlets

2. Using a string line as a guide, position brackets to support drop outlets and gutter joint

Now comes the easy part of the job – putting up the brackets to support the new gutters, and assembling each guttering run.

Start by hanging a plumbline from the fascia directly above each splash block position, to determine where the gutter drop outlets will be positioned. Then screw a bracket to the fascia to support the outlet (or the end of the adjacent gutter length; which you do depends on the design of the system you're installing). Set this as low on the fascia as possible, to ensure that the run has a fall from its highest point. However, to avoid rainwater splashing out of the gutter as it runs off the roof at this point, don't set it any more than 2in below the bottom edge of the roof covering.

Now put up a second bracket at the opposite end of the run to give the correct fall, and set up a taut string line from it to the first bracket. The ideal fall along the run should be about 1in in 12 ft but you should check the manufacturer's recommendations for a precise figure. Where the run turns corners, drive nails into the fascia to carry the string line round them. If two runs discharge into a centrally positioned downspout, set up string lines in both directions.

With the string line in place, start attaching brackets to the fascia at the recommended spacings. Generally speaking there should be a bracket

beneath (or close to) each gutter joint. Drill pilot holes and secure the brackets with rustproof screws.

With some systems, the gutter connectors, corners and outlets are screwed directly to the fascia. If this is the case, attach these next.

You can then start inserting whole gutter lengths. Position each length so its rear edge is underneath the lip of the roof, and clip it into its bracket. Join on the next length, using connectors. With some systems you have to form notches in the edge of the gutter to take the clips; use a file, if this is the case.

★ **TIP**

As you link the lengths of guttering together, don't forget to leave an expansion gap of about ⅜in at each connection. Plastic gutters expand and contract slightly as the temperature changes, and may creak alarmingly as they do unless they can move freely at their joints.

Where you have to cut guttering to length, use the end of another section as a saw guide and cut the piece with a hacksaw or fine-toothed general-purpose saw. File off any rough edges.

Add corner pieces as required where the run turns and put on

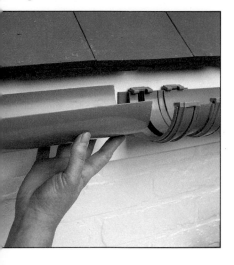

3. Position the drop outlet and then start inserting whole gutter lengths along the run

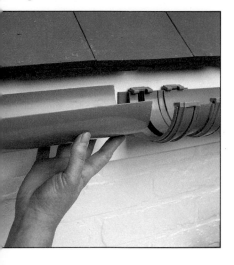

4. With the rear edge of the gutter under the lip of the roof, clip each length into its bracket

end caps at each end of the run to contain the rainwater.

⭐ **TIP**

If you are putting up new metal guttering, seal the connection between lengths with a bead of caulking. Test all the connections on the ground before you set the new guttering in position. Lift up the lowest shingles to nail in strap hangers and put a daub of caulking around each nail before folding back the shingle and hanging the guttering.

5 Installing new downspouts

To complete your new rainwater system, all that remains is to make up and install the downspout runs.

Drop a plumbline from the fascia board immediately below each outlet, to help ensure that you position the run vertically, and lift up the elbow so you can mark the position of the top of the first downspout length on the wall. Some systems include double elbows of a standard size with projections of 4, 6, 9 or 12 in; with others, you have to make up an offset from two 135° elbows and a short length of pipe, slotting the pieces together. With the elbow and the first length of pipe held in place, mark the positions of the screw holes through the downspout bracket and secure it in place. Insert wallplugs, and secure with rust-proof screws.

Lift up and attach subsequent lengths in the same way, leaving a ¼in expansion gap within each socket connection. Check that each length is truly vertical before you mark the screw holes.

Add extra brackets halfway down sections over 6ft long, for extra support.

At the bottom of the run, cut the last section to length and add an elbow to direct the water onto the splash block away from the house.

1. If an elbow is not required, use a simple connector to link gutter and downpipe

■ Options

Cast iron systems in traditional styles may be used for older or period buildings

Plastic gutters and downspouts are available in brown, green and grey as well as in black and white

Plastic rainwater systems come in a variety of cross-sections

CHECKLIST

Materials
bricks (approx 200 for a
free-standing arch)
sand, masonry cement
for mortar
cement and aggregate
wood scraps and planks
for supports
wooden wedges
string

Tools
spade for mixing mortar
mixing board
trowels
jigsaw or saber saw
tape measure
ruler
level
straightedge
pair of calipers or dividers

See Skills Guide pp. 117,
123, 125 and 133

Brick Arches

A brick arch can add a touch of elegance to your garden. You can build one over a gate, set into a wall or made into a free-standing feature or centerpiece. It is also a lot easier to build than it looks.

If you've acquired any of the skills of bricklaying, you'll find it's surprisingly easy to construct a brick arch. Like any other brickwork, you'll need concrete foundations for the vertical 'piers' and these must be capable of supporting a wall about 6ft 6in high, though you can alter this height to suit your situation if you want.

The secret of building a successful arch lies in making the wooden former or 'arch center'. This forms the shape of the arch and supports the bricks while you lay them. Once all the bricks are in place the structure is self-supporting and you can remove the former as soon as the mortar has set.

The arch works because the bricks are wedged together by the mortar – the weight of the bricks is directed around the curve of the arch and ends up resting entirely on the piers. There is a little sideways force, though, which is why the piers need to be fairly substantial – at least one and a half bricks long, and preferably two (as in this project). A flatter arch has a much greater sideways force and the piers need to be even wider.

As long as you bear this in mind, you can adapt the project to create many different arch shapes. Popular shapes are the segmental arch – so called because its shape is a segment of a circle – and a pointed arch ('Gothic' style).

When you choose the location for your arch, think about the type of bricks to use. If it's to go in a rustic setting, perhaps with creepers growing around the arch, choose irregular rough-finished bricks which you can buy second-hand.

DESIGNS FOR A BRICK ARCH

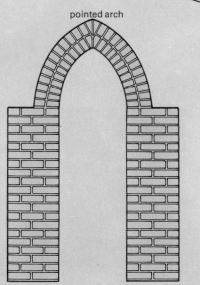

A freestanding arch with a semi-circular shape must be supported on two piers. The arch has two courses of brick to give it substance and rigidity and the piers must be at least two bricks wide. Most of the weight of the arch pushes down but there is some sideways 'spring' so the piers must not be made too narrow.

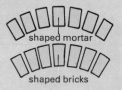

shaped mortar

shaped bricks

There are two ways to make the arch – by shaping either the mortar or the bricks. You can buy specially-shaped bricks, but they are expensive

pointed arch

segmental arch

A pointed arch is built in much the same way as the semi-circular ('Romanesque') arch. Take pains to measure and mark the arch former accurately to ensure that you get good results.

A segmental arch is shallow and exerts considerable sideways thrust. It is best built into a brick wall or supported between two buildings rather than on narrow piers.

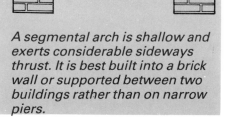

LAY THE FOUNDATIONS

The piers have to support quite a weight and need to be built on proper foundations. Mark the positions of the piers on the ground and excavate to at least 2ft – more if the ground is soft – and about 4in wider than the pier on all sides. Mix up six parts mixed aggregate to one of cement and pour the concrete into the hole. Level off the top and leave to set. In hot, dry weather, cover the concrete with damp rags to prevent it from drying out.

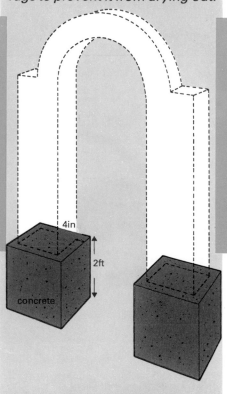

4in

2ft

concrete

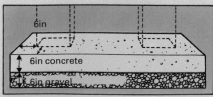

6in

6in concrete

6in gravel

If the foundations are part of a larger slab you can make them with 6in of gravel topped with 6in of concrete – the area of the slab will give sufficient support.

77

MAKE THE FORMER

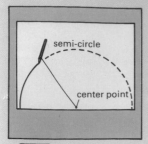

Construct your arch center from two semi-circles of plywood. Cut out with a jig saw.

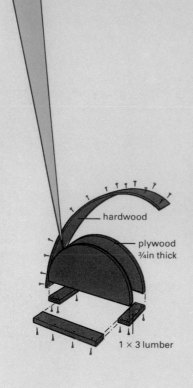

hardwood

plywood ¾in thick

1 × 3 lumber

Alternatively, make the sides from quarter-circles cut from scraps and nailed to cross pieces

The arch center must be sturdy enough to support the weight of bricks. Use ¾in plywood for the sides, hardboard for the top and 1 × 3 lumber for the base.

BUILD THE FIRST PIER

Mix up 1 part masonry cement to 4½ parts sand, for the mortar. There is no need for a vapor barrier unless the arch butts against the house wall. Work out the bond depending on the size of the pier, and for a two-brick pier use the scheme below. Lay a thin bed of mortar to start then, as you lay each course, spread an even layer of mortar on top ready for the next course. Butter the sides and ends of the bricks before you lay them, and keep the mortar joints even – about ½in thick.

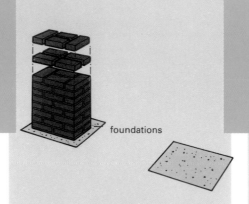

foundations

As you lay the bricks, constantly check that the pier is vertical. Tap bricks back into line with the handle of your trowel

The pier should be high enough for you to walk under – 6ft 6in is about right. If you are putting in a gate, build it to the height required and set the hinges into the mortar courses as you go.

BUILD THE SECOND PIER

Score the outline of the pier in a bed of mortar. Use the former as a spacer and a straightedge to mark the front line.

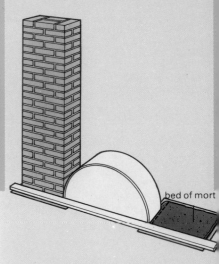

bed of mort

As you build, use a wooden rod – its length equal to the distance between the piers – to check the span is constant

Build up the second pier – remember to start off with the same brick bond. If the mortar is starting to 'go off' you can point the piers before starting on the arch (see section 10).

5 PROP UP ARCH CENTER

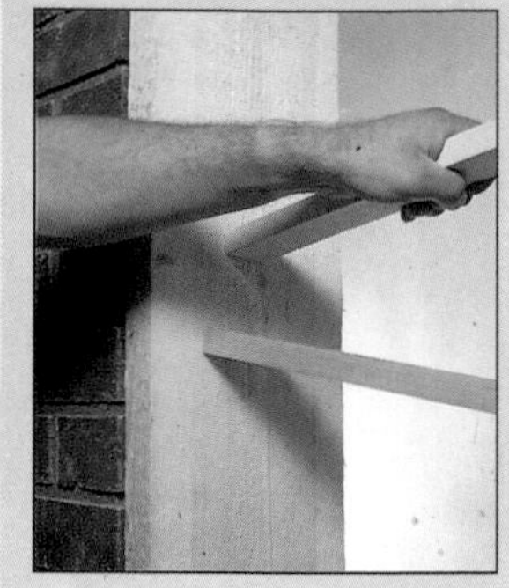

Erect former supports with strips of wood wedged between the piers. Don't push too hard: Level the former on the top

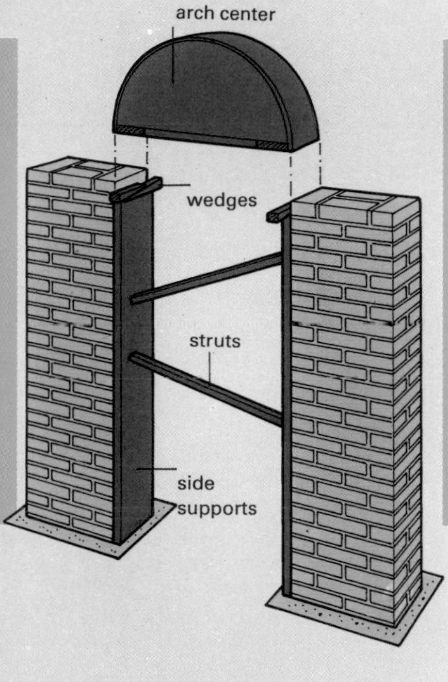

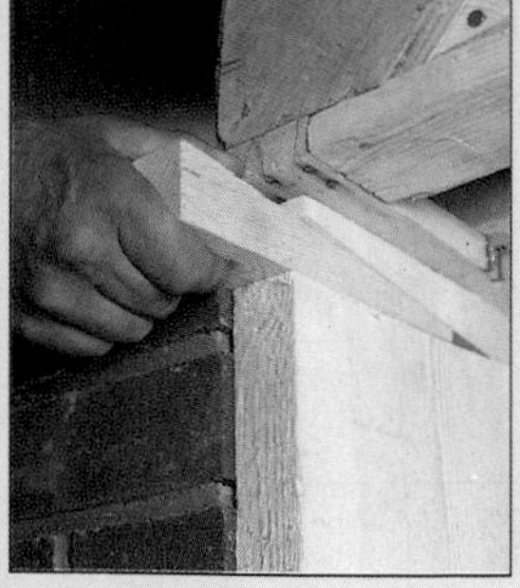

Use wooden wedges to make the final adjustments at each side. Make sure the arch former is precisely horizontal and firm

Use planks as side supports and cut them slightly shorter than the pier – use the wedges to raise the center to the correct height. Add packing pieces to the wedges if the formwork is wobbly or unstable.

6 MARK BRICK SPACING

To work out the position and spacing of the bricks, first stand a brick at the center of the formwork. Set your calipers to the width of the brick, plus ¼in for mortar, and step this along the edge of the arch to the last whole brick needed to reach the pier. Measure the gap that's left, divide by the number of bricks on that side and widen the calipers by this amount. The calipers should now step out a whole number of bricks – plus mortar gaps – on each side. Accuracy at this stage is crucial.

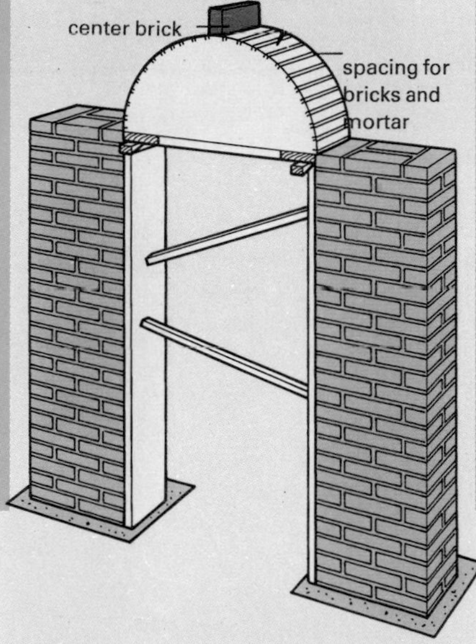

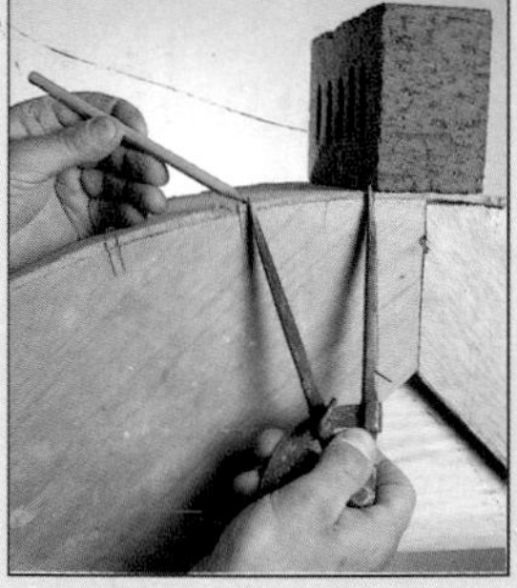

With the calipers set to the correct spacing, mark the position of the bricks and the gaps for the mortar

For structural and visual reasons, the bricks of the arch should be laid symmetrically with a whole brick in the center. When marking, position a brick in the center then mark spacings to the piers.

7 LAY THE FIRST ARCH COURSE

Butter the mortar onto the brick in a wedge shape. Leave a gap at the bottom so mortar stays clear of the former

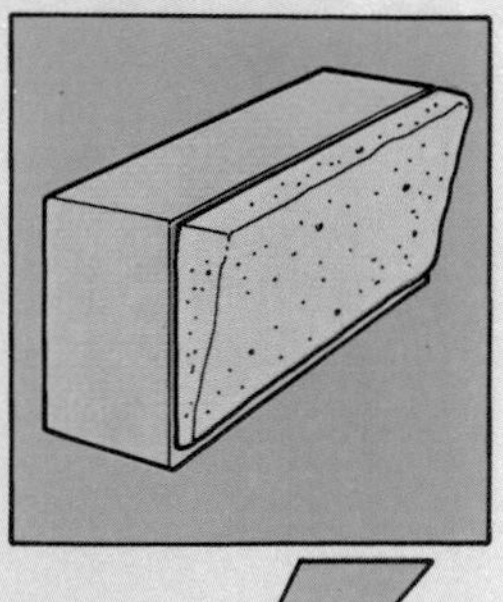

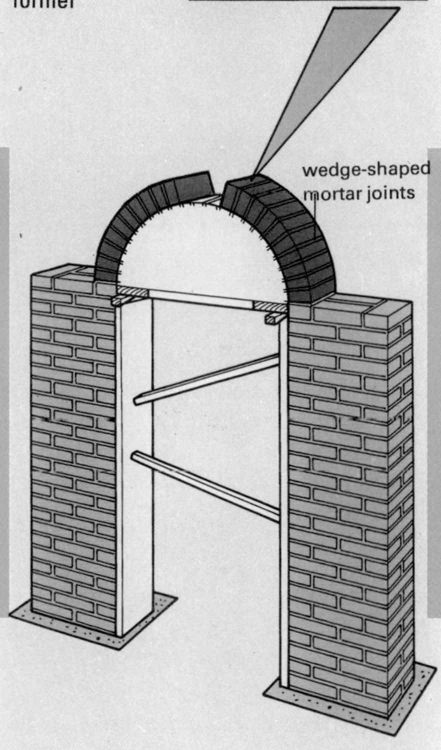

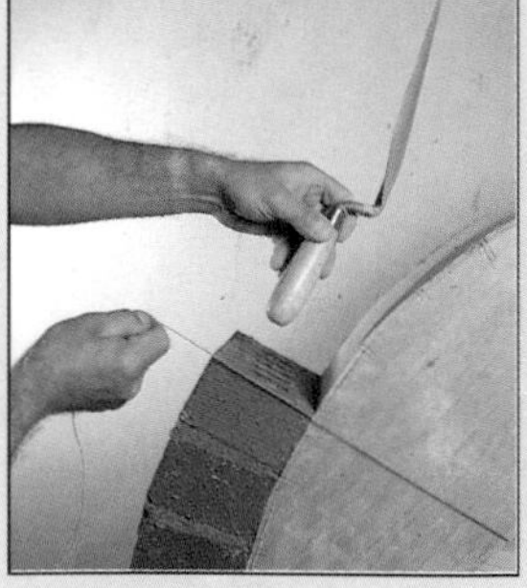

Use string tied to the center of the arch to help you align the bricks to the correct angle. Align with your marks

Lay the bricks working from each pier in turn, aligning carefully with your marks. Stop when there are three bricks still to go. Check as you go that the face of the arch is vertical and that the curve is even.

LAY THE CENTER BRICKS

Dry-lay the last three bricks to recheck the spacing then ease them carefully into place. The last brick must be central

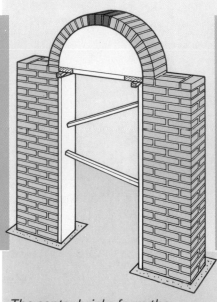

The center bricks form the 'keystone' of the arch: if you've marked accurately, they should all fit.

LAY THE SECOND COURSE

Try to keep the same thickness of mortar for the second course of bricks. Use the string as before

Lay the second course in the same way, but stagger the courses or increase the joint thicknesses.

FINISH OFF

Leave the mortar to set then carefully remove the wedges and lower the arch center. Release the struts and remove the props

pointing

Use a small trowel to point the brickwork. A raked-out profile looks very attractive with this type of arch

Leave the mortar to set before pointing. This may take anything from 10 minutes to three hours depending on the temperature and the porosity of the bricks, but leave it until it is fairly firm as the job will be easier.

Simple Wooden Sundeck

Enjoy the sunshine in your backyard on this simple ranch-style sundeck. It's easy to build, not too costly, adaptable to all sizes and very stylish.

Compared to the cost and work involved in building a patio, this solid softwood sundeck works out cost-effective – and gives you a made-to-measure touch of originality.

The design is simplicity itself. Standard softwood boards (thoroughly treated with preservative) give you the main supports and posts, planed softwood boards provide the decking. Thick posts – built-up from thinner members and

sunk into the ground – and a ledger strip attached to the house wall provide all the support that's necessary. You could also use redwood or cedar with their natural resistance to decay. You'll need surprisingly few tools and skills too – there are no complicated joints anywhere in the entire structure.

The sundeck featured on these pages is 11ft 6in long and 6ft 6in deep. The balustrading provides plenty of raised surfaces for displaying plants. If you want to alter the area of the decking, use the illustrations to work out what you need to do to fit your needs.

CHECKLIST

Tools
spade or post hole borer
hand saw, backsaw, power saw
bevel edge chisel
drill and bits
hammer and nail punch
level/tape measure

Materials
wood preservative
vapor barrier
four masonry bolts
3 and 4in galvanized nails
4in casing nails
200ft of 2 × 6
130ft of 1 × 6
60ft of 2 × 4

See Skills Guide
pp. 110, 112, 116, 122, 132 and 137

A SIZE AND SHAPE TO SUIT YOUR YARD

The construction may look very complicated but is in fact quite straightforward. Your major difficulty will lie in working out what you need and cutting it to length. The sundeck featured on these pages is 11ft 6in long and 6ft 6in deep – ample for most needs. If you want to change the size and shape from that shown, aim to keep the same spans between all posts (D and C).

Work out the ideal size for your house, then use the following assembly line illustrations to work out what you actually need. Bear in mind that the main frame is formed by the ledger strip, the beams and the posts (D and C): lengths and spacings determine the lengths of the other components. You could complete it piecemeal fashion but it pays to make a clear plan.

Get a clear idea of the size you want then draw a scale plan. Use 2 × 4 lumber for ledger strip, joists and beams, as well as for infills **G** and **H**

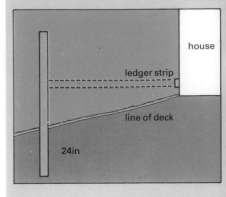

Vary lengths of posts **D** to suit slopes

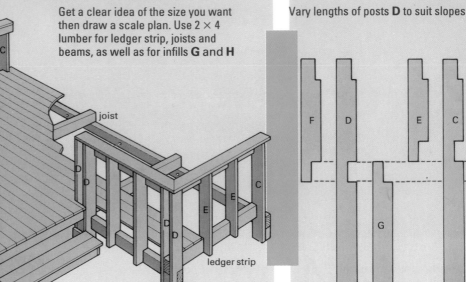

Mark the height of the notches, then use scrap from the joist or beam to mark the size of the cutout. Cut with a saw and chisel

The structure consists of a ledger strip measuring 2 × 9 bolted to the house wall. Joists measuring 2 × 4 run from the ledger strip to the front of the sundeck where they meet the corner and intermediate posts (D). The posts are made from smaller section timbers nailed together and notched to accommodate the joists. You can use the joists to accurately locate the distance of the posts from the ledger strip. Though they're nailed to the posts, the joists actually rest on a beam. Once this main frame is complete, the decking, the rail posts (E) and the top rail

(A and B) can be added. You'll need to plan a rectangular site, marking in the corner posts and intermediate support posts. For the size illustrated here, you'll need four sets of main support posts (D) along the long side plus another set to support the step. You'll need an intermediate post (C) mid-point along one side and at either end of the ledger strip. If you alter the sizes, aim to provide posts at a maximum of 4ft intervals around the perimeter of the sundeck area. Use the following instructions to get a clear picture of what's involved.

For the sundeck size shown here, you need 10 posts **D** of 1 × 6 and 5 infills **G** of 2 × 4. You need 6 short rails **E** and 6 long rails **F** plus 4 posts **C** and one special infill **H** for the intermediate post. Cut the notches in the positions shown.

PREPARE THE POSTS

MARKING THE SITE ▼2

Before attaching the wallplate, apply a vapor barrier to the back

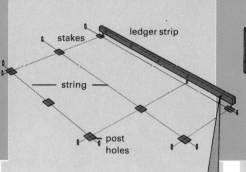

Secure the ledger strip, then mark the site using stakes and string. Measure to locate the post holes

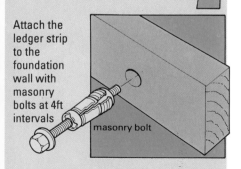

Attach the ledger strip to the foundation wall with masonry bolts at 4ft intervals

Mark the position and height you want against the foundation wall, then attach a ledger strip with masonry bolts. Set out the site with care. See Skills Guide pp. 130, 137.

SINK THE POST SUPPORTS ▼3

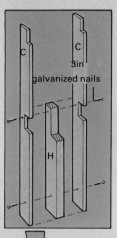

Intermediate side posts must include a notch for the side joist at a higher level – in all other respects it is like any other post and built as shown. Soak with preservative

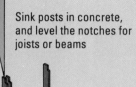

Sink posts in concrete, and level the notches for joists or beams

Dig the post holes, then level the notches with the ledger strip. Set posts on a gravel base, apply a preservative, then fill in with concrete. Check with a level, then brace

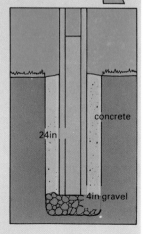

Dig the post holes to the required depth using a spade or a post hole borer. Set the posts so that the notches are level.

ATTACH BEAMS AND JOISTS ▼4

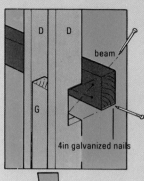

Attach the beams by toe nailing: they should be level with the ledger strip and level with post infills **G**. Joists slot between the uprights **D**

Cut and nail on the beams first, then attach the joists. Slip side joists into notches

Toe nail into the joists by nailing through uprights **D** at an angle to avoid any movement

Beams and joists complete the main frame – nail beams into the notches in the posts, then attach the joists by slipping them between the uprights and toe nailing. Make sure that the concrete in which the posts are set has had time to cure thoroughly before nailing.

83

ADD POSTS AND RAILS

Once the top rails are in place, add the posts (**E**, **F**) at regular intervals between the support posts. Check for level and nail secure

LAY THE DECKING

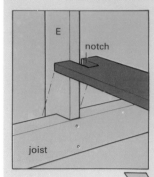

Cut out the decking using 2 × 6 boards. You must notch some to fit around the 'baluster' posts

ADD THE STEP

Nail the step supports to the posts then add short decking. The step can rest on the ground

Add the top rail then add the posts

Cut decking to length and lay them out with regular spaces between, then secure

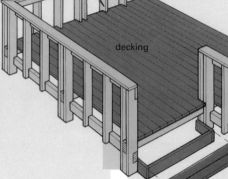

Direct measure the length of the step to fit between posts

decking

step

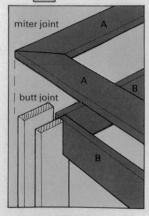

miter joint

butt joint

Cut the top rail (**A**) to full length, then cut 45° miters on the ends. Nail **B** on to the ends of the posts then nail **A** to **B** and to the top of the posts

*Attach the top rail – made from **A** and **B** – to the tops of the posts. With this in place, you can then add the 'baluster' posts **E** and **F**, nailing them to beams and rail.*

Starting at the house wall, lay out the decking (with spacers). Use 4in nails.

Build up the step using scraps. Use decking for the step surface, joist scraps for support.

★ *An easy way to dig the post holes*

You can rent manual post hole borers, but a gasoline driven borer will make light work of the job. Rental companies can supply them. You must take special care to avoid underground pipes or electric cable lines.

Wooden Fences

Wooden fences are a popular choice for marking property boundaries. They come in a wide range of styles, don't cost the earth and are quick and easy to put up. All you have to do is take the measurements and order the right materials.

Every property needs secure boundaries, and fences do the job extremely well. They're cheaper than masonry walls, are quick to erect and are preferable to hedges, which can take years to grow sufficiently to form a continuous barrier.

There are two basic types of wooden fence. Panel fences are built up by setting prefabricated rectangular panels between the posts. Rail fences have horizontal rails running between the posts – a simple post-and-rail fence. Vertical boards can be nailed to the rails to improve privacy by being set close together, while spaced verticals give a paling or picket fence. You can create all sorts of variations by adding extra rails for example to form ranch-style fencing, and you can top any type with open trelliswork to improve privacy and train climbing plants.

There's nothing to stop you making up a fence from scratch, but most people prefer to purchase everything from a lumber yard or garden center as pre-assembled panels. This method has the advantage that all the wood is pre-treated with preservative, and most of the time consuming assembly work has been done.

1 What the job involves

You don't need any special skills to put up a new fence. All the job requires is careful measuring and neat workmanship to ensure professional looking results.

Whatever type of fencing you decide to erect, the job breaks down into three main stages. You have to:

● clear the site, which often means removing the remains of an existing fence, wall or hedge

● set the posts in the ground, either in concrete or using metal fence spikes

● fill in between them with prefabricated panels or rails to which boards or pickets are then nailed

● on very rare cases you may require permission to build a fence, particularly if you live in a planned community where you back onto common space. There are generally restrictions which regulate the height of fences around swimming pools to ensure safety. Check to see what the restrictions are in your area as they vary from place to place.

CHECKLIST

Tools
crowbar and old saw
spade
post-hole borer
steel tape measure
stakes and string line
level
claw hammer
hand saw
plane

Materials
fence posts
fence panels or
    rails and boards
fence brackets
galvanized nails
wood preservative
coping and post caps
concrete

 See Skills Guide
p. 137

BEFORE YOU START

● Make sure you know exactly where the boundary line is. This is obvious when an old fence, wall or hedge is being removed, but may be less certain on properties with open frontages or wild back yards.

● Check the ownership of any fence you intend to replace. If you are in any doubt, your property deeds should make this clear.

● Apply for building permission if it is required. If you add trelliswork to the top of a high fence, you may unwittingly breach local height restrictions.

● Choose the type of fencing you want. Panel fencing is generally cheaper than board fencing, and is quicker and easier to put up, but some types are less durable.

● Measure the site carefully, so you can work out exactly how many posts and other components you will need.

! WATCH OUT FOR

● Sloping or uneven sites. On slopes, post and rail fences are easier to use than panel types, since the rails can follow the slope of the ground. You can use panel fencing

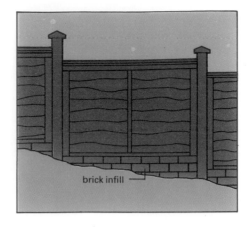

You will need to construct an infill panel between the posts if your fence is on sloping ground

only if you form steps down the slope and fill them in.

● Underground concrete. Old fence posts may have been set in concrete which is very difficult to excavate. The answer is to alter your starting point so the new fence positions fall between the old ones. If the new fence is replacing a boundary wall, the only solution is to dig up all the old foundations before you begin.

Vertical board and panel fencing are easy to erect. Some types use brackets and clamps for assembly.

2 Prepare the

In most situations, your first job will be to remove whatever is marking your boundary at present – a dilapidated fence, a crumbling wall or an old hedge.

An old **fence** may, quite literally, be falling down. If this is the case, simply tear out the old panels, boards or rails with a crowbar; then pry the old posts out of the ground. If a boarded fence is not completely rotten, saw through the rails next to the posts first to make dismantling easier.

It may be tempting to save the wood for some other project, but this is worth doing only if the wood is dry, sound and free from decay. It's better to pile it up neatly and have a bonfire – well away from boundaries, buildings and any overhanging trees. If you don't have room for a fire, rent a dumpster to get rid of everything.

★ TIP

Pull out stubborn posts using a simple lever and fulcrum arrangement. Tie one end of an old post to the base of the stuck post just above ground level. Then set a pile of bricks beneath the lever next to the post, and press down on the other end of the lever to lift

Where a masonry **wall** is being replaced by a fence, demolish the above-ground brickwork with a

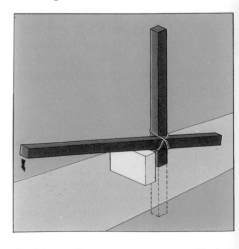

Stubborn fence posts can easily be removed using a simple lever and fulcrum method

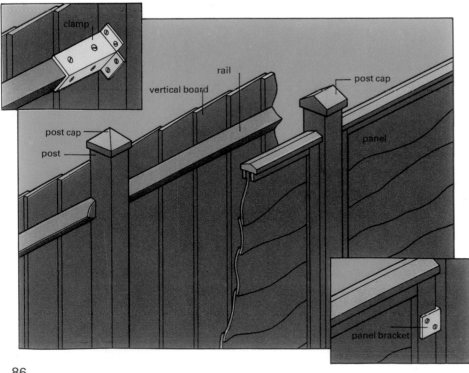

boundary

3 Set the first post

Once you have prepared the site for your new fence, the next task is to set the first fence post in position at one end of the run.

Set up a string line to indicate the position of the complete run. This ensures that you don't wander off line as you work.

You can then dig the first hole. For fences less than about 4ft high you need to bury about 18in of post in the ground; for taller fences increase this to 2ft. Make the hole 6in or so deeper to allow for some gravel beneath the foot of the post. This prevents water from accumulating there and encouraging decay. Either cut a neat hole about 9in square with a spade, or use a post-hole borer.

⭐ **TIP**

Rent a post-hole borer if you have a lot of holes to make or the soil is very hard. This works like a larger auger or plug cutter, removing a core of soil neatly and easily, saving time and effort.

Ram some gravel or crushed stone in the bottom of the hole and set the post in place, checking that the right amount is set below ground level. Then prop it upright with two braces, pack in more gravel and soil to within about 6in of the surface and add a collar of concrete, tamped down firmly round the post. Finish off the surface of the concrete with a slight slope away from the foot of the post, so rainwater is encouraged to run off. Check once more that the post is truly vertical.

You may need to secure the first fence post next to the house or garage wall. The building's foundations will prevent you from setting the post in the ground, so cut it off short and attach it to the wall instead. Use 4in bolts for this – two about 3ft apart on short posts, three on taller ones. Drill the holes in the post first, then enlarge the first 1in or so to allow you to recess the bolt heads; otherwise they'll obstruct the edge of the panel or last board. Mark the bolt positions through the post holes,

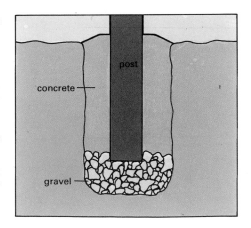

1. Position the post in the center of the hole and nail supporting pieces of wood to each side

drill the holes with a large-diameter drill bit and secure the post in place, tightening the bolts in their counterbores with a socket wrench.

With panel fencing, you may prefer to set one post in place at a time, then set the panel between it and the previous post before setting the next one in place. With rail types, where the post spacing is not so critical, it's often better to set all the posts in place in one session, to enable the concrete to set thoroughly. On level ground, check as you position each post that all the tops are level.

Stand the post *on gravel, then pour in the concrete, shaping the surface away from the post*

1. Remove the post caps and copings from the old fence and pull out the nails with a claw hammer

sledgehammer if it hasn't fallen over already. Take care not to injure passers-by if the wall borders on a sidewalk. Then dig up the old foundations, and load all the debris into a dumpster unless you have some use for a lot of rubble.

Cut an old **hedge** down to about 6in above ground level, then dig out the individual stumps. The short stem you left will help give extra leverage. Pull out stubborn posts using a simple lever and fulcrum arrangement. Tie an old post to the base of the fence post, then set bricks or a concrete block beneath. Press down on the old post to lift the fence post out.

2. Use a crowbar to pry the panel or vertical boards away from the fence post

4 Add the panels

If you're putting up a panel fence, this is the easy – and most rewarding – part of the job. All you need is a hammer, a fistful of galvanized nails ... and someone to help steady the panels.

Lift up the panel between the first pair of posts, and check that it fits snugly between them. If it's a tight fit, you can plane or saw a fraction off the edge of the panel. To stop the bottom of the fence from rotting, you should have a gap of about 2in between it and the soil; use scraps of wood as props. Check that the panel is central on the face of the post, and drive nails through the

1. Check that the panel fits between the two fence posts with a small gap either side for the bracket

edging strips to secure it. Use three nails per edge for fences up to about 3ft high, five otherwise.

Put up the remaining panels in the same way, checking that their tops are level on flat ground and that the step-down between panels is even on slopes.

As an alternative to nailing the panels to the posts, in some cases you can use small galvanized brackets. These are U-shaped, and are nailed to the inner face of posts; use two per edge on low fences, three or four on high ones. When you've attached them, lower or spring the panel into position and drive nails into the panels through the pre-drilled holes in the brackets – ideally from both sides of the fence.

At the end of the run, you are likely to have to cut the final panel down in width. Pry off the edging strips from both sides of one edge and reposition them to give a panel of the required width. Then saw down the panel next to the repositioned edge strips.

★ **TIP**

Save the scraps when you cut down sections of panels because they may be useful in the future to match up if you have to make some repairs to a damaged panel.

5 Putting up

If you're putting up a post-and-rail fence, the next job is to add the rails between the posts, ready to receive the boards or pickets.

Traditional fences of this type have the rails set in mortises in the sides of the posts. They therefore have to be set in place as the next post is positioned, and are secured to the post by a nail driven through each rail end. It can be tricky putting up a fence in this way, since you must keep the mortises accurately in line as you place the posts.

It's simpler to use special rail brackets made of galvanized steel, which are nailed first to the rail end and then to the post. Or simply nail the rails to the face of the post. If you use brackets it is easier in the future to replace a rail if it is damaged or becomes rotten. Don't forget to use rustproof nails. You can simply slot the new rail into the bracket, or, if you are repairing a fence that originally used mortise joints, a rail clamp is easiest to use.

On a vertical boarded fence, the next job is to add a gravel board between each pair of posts. The object of this is not only to hold back gravel, soil or anything else from the boundary, but also to protect the vulnerable end grain of the boards from moisture and decay. Nail small cleats to the inner face of each post, then cut the gravel board to length to fit between the posts and nail it to the cleats so its rear edge is vertically below the face of the rails.

Now you can start adding the boards to the rails. If you're using tapered boards, cut the first board to length (if necessary) and stand it on the gravel board with its thick edge next to the post. Drive 2in galvanized nails through its face into the rail behind, which you can steady with your other hand to prevent 'bounce' as you hammer in the nails. Position the next board so its thick edge overlaps the thin edge of the previous board by about 1½in, and repeat the process.

Use a level after every fourth or fifth board to check that you're putting them up vertically. Continue in this way until you reach the next post; cut down the final board in

2. Remove the panel, then nail the brackets to the fence posts, at the top and bottom

3. Slide or spring the panel between the brackets then nail in place on both sides

rails and boards 6 Finish off   Options

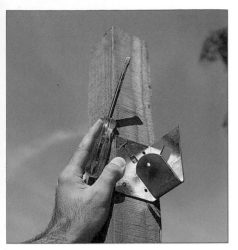

1. Screw the rail bracket to the fence post, with the edge against the back edge of the post

1. Attach the post caps, using two nails in the top of each one to stop them from rotating

Double rail fencing sets rails on alternate sides of the post for greater privacy in your yard

width if necessary to fill the gap. Reverse it so its thick edge is against the post. Repeat the whole process for the other bays that make up the run.

Follow a similar sequence for picket fences, this time using scrap as a spacer between individual pickets. Once again, check at regular intervals that the pickets are truly vertical using a level — this is especially important on sloping ground.

Finish off your new fence by adding coping strips to the top of the rails and caps to all the posts.

Coping strips and post caps help stop water penetration, especially of vulnerable end grain, and so make your fence last longer. Cut the bevelled copings to length and nail them to the top edge of the fence. Then nail a cap to the top of each post.

Finish off your new fence by giving all the woodwork a further coat of preservative. Even though the wood should have been pretreated, this precaution will lengthen its life still further.

Panel and vertical boarded fences are the most popular types, but you can create several alternatives if you wish. Most are variations on the basic post-and-rail design.

Ranch-style fencing is particularly easy to put up. Set your posts anything from 4 to 8ft apart, and then nail on horizontal planks with a gap in between. The plank width can be anything from 4in up to 9in, while the spacing is entirely up to you. Generally a gap equal to the plank width looks best.

Double rail fencing is a variant on the ranch style, and has the advantage of improving privacy considerably. Planks are attached to one side of the posts as for a ranch-style fence; then a second set is added on the other side of the posts, aligned with the gaps.

As an alternative to sinking your fence posts in concrete, you can erect them using metal fence spikes. These come in two sizes — a 2ft long spike for fences up to 4ft high and a 2ft 6in version for fences up to 6ft high. They're ideal on hard, fairly fine soil, but it's difficult to ensure that they are driven truly vertically in rocky types of soil, which is vital.

2. Slide the rail into the brackets between the posts and screw it into place

2. Finish your fence with a coat of wood preservative — preferably one that is not harmful to plants

Erect a Greenhouse

Any enthusiastic gardener will appreciate the facilities a greenhouse has to offer. Even a small one will keep a garden well supplied with young plants and allow delicate fruit and vegetables to be grown irrespective of weather conditions. Aluminum greenhouses are easy to erect, needing only basic skills.

Most greenhouses are rectangular in shape with vertical or sloping sides. They come in free-standing or lean-to versions, the latter being particularly useful in a small garden where space is limited. Octagonal free-standing greenhouses are also available. Although there is a range of sizes to choose from, something in the region of 6 × 8ft should suit most gardeners.

Some greenhouses are fully glazed from ground to ridge, while others may have solid lower sides, and which you choose will depend on the types of plant you intend growing and

how much light they require. You can choose between a wood-framed greenhouse and an aluminum-framed version. The former are sometimes cheaper and more aesthetically pleasing, but they do require regular treatment to protect the wood against decay and insect attack. However, the latter are virtually maintenance free and will last considerably longer.

Most greenhouse suppliers offer an erection service, but the job is not a difficult one and well within the capabilities of most people – few tools are required to complete the task.

1 What the job involves

Although the exact method of assembling a greenhouse will vary from one manufacturer to another, the procedure is basically the same. Wood frame greenhouses will almost certainly be supplied as ready-assembled end and side panels ready for bolting together and glazing; aluminum-framed versions will come as a collection of extrusions which are bolted together to make a framework and then glazed.

To erect an aluminum-framed greenhouse you'll need to:
● mark out the position of the greenhouse on the ground.
● level the site, making sure the ground is well compacted if a prefabricated base is being used. Alternatively, dig out a hole for a concrete slab foundation, or a concrete perimeter foundation or brick footings.
● Assemble the prefabricated base, if using, and anchor it to the ground, or build a concrete or brick base.
● Assemble the framework for each side including any vents.
● Assemble the end frameworks.
● Join the sides to the ends and add the ridge bar, roofing bars and any vents.
● Assemble the door framework and hang it with its track at the appropriate end of the greenhouse.
● Insert the glazing strips and add the panes of glass using the spring clips provided.

CHECKLIST

steel tape measure
level
plumb line
screwdriver
pliers
open-ended, adjustable
    wrench
sharp knife
gloves

See Skills Guide
pp. 133–134

BEFORE YOU START

● Decide on the greenhouse position – it must not be shaped by nearby hedges, trees, fences or buildings, exposed to strong winds or be sited in a low spot in the garden where cold air might collect on a winter night. To receive as much sunlight as possible during winter, the ridge of the greenhouse should run east-west, and a lean-to version should be erected against a south-facing wall. Keeping the greenhouse close to the house will allow electricity and water to be added easily.

● Check with your local zoning department about zoning approval. This probably won't be needed but you might as well check.

● Make sure the ground is well compacted. Build a concrete or brick foundation if necessary, and check that it is square and level.

● Unpack the greenhouse, checking the parts against the delivery note; inform the suppliers immediately if any part is damaged or missing.

● If erecting the greenhouse on a concrete or brick base, make sure you have a supply of suitable screws and plugs, or expanding bolts, to secure it in place.

● Clear a flat area nearby where the aluminum sections can be laid out and assembled.

● Organize help to position the completed sections of framework.

! WATCH OUT FOR

● Forgotten bolts. Check the instructions carefully to see if bolts need inserting beforehand.

● Lack of space round the finished greenhouse. There should be enough room for cleaning.

● Sharp edges on the glass panes. Always wear thick gloves.

An aluminum greenhouse comes in a large box – unpack it and check the contents carefully.

An aluminum greenhouse kit comes as a flat pack, usually comprising a bolt-together base with a variety of bars and posts.

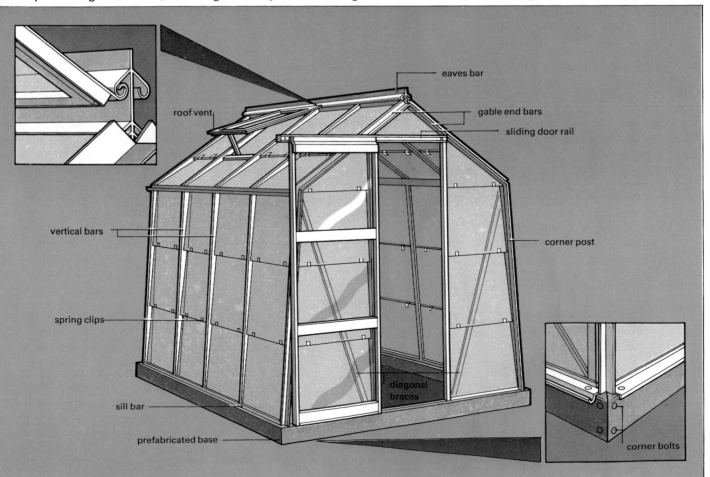

eaves bar

gable end bars

sliding door rail

roof vent

vertical bars

corner post

spring clips

diagonal braces

sill bar

prefabricated base

corner bolts

2 Build base framework

The diagonal measurements of the frame should be equal if it is square. Use a tape or string.

It is essential to ensure that the base for the greenhouse is both level and square. If it is not, the framework will be out of true and the glass will not fit properly.

A concrete or brick base may need wooden shims placed underneath the framework. Make sure the wood is treated with preservative before installation.

A prefabricated base may be made of aluminum or galvanized steel sections which simply bolt together at the corners to form a rigid framework.

Assemble the framework loosely and lift it into position. Align the framework and use a level to check that the sides and ends are level – if necessary, dig out beneath the frame members until they are level. Don't add material beneath them since this will not be compacted sufficiently and may cause movement later.

Once the frame has been leveled, square it up by checking the diagonal measurements between the corners. If the frame is square, the measurements will be equal. Then tighten the bolts, but check the diagonals again afterwards in case anything has moved.

Finally, anchor the frame to the ground by driving in the pins provided or digging pockets in the ground for its bolt-on feet.

3 Construct the sides

Assemble the side framework flat on the ground, adding the diagonal braces to hold it rigid.

When assembling the side frames, make sure you identify the correct sections to use. Often they may be similar to others in the greenhouse. Although the precise arrangement may vary slightly from one make of greenhouse to another, the side frames are likely to comprise a horizontal eaves bar, a horizontal sill bar and a number of vertical bars that join the two. In addition, there will be two diagonal braces, one at each end. Lay these out on the ground in their relative positions.

Pay particular attention to the way in which the aluminum sections are orientated, i.e. the slots that accept the glazing strips should face outwards and the diagonal bracing bars will be on the inside. In addition, there may be flanges on the sill and/or eaves bars that must be on the outside or inside of the assembled greenhouse.

Slide the bolts into the upright, remembering to include those that hold the diagonal braces. Then loosely bolt together the sill bar, eaves bar and uprights. Finally, add the diagonal braces, making sure the bolts at their ends are pushed through the sill and eaves bars from the outside so that they do not obstruct the glass.

Repeat the procedure for the second side frame and stand or lay the assemblies out of the way.

4 Build gable ends

1. Cast-aluminum brackets may be used to join the gable end bars at the ridge and to the corner posts.

The method of assembling the gable end frames of the greenhouse is essentially the same for both ends, although there will be a slight difference between the assemblies due to one having a door opening. As with the side frames, identify the various parts beforehand and lay them out on the ground.

The gable end frame comprises a triangular top plate or angle bracket, a pair of gable end bars, a pair of corner posts, two gusset plates or brackets that fit between the gable end bars and the corner posts, a sill bar, a horizontal brace, two diagonal braces and at least two vertical bars.

Begin construction by bolting the gable end bars to the top plate or bracket, followed by the corner posts to the gable end bars using the plates or brackets provided. Make sure the corner posts are set the correct way around, that is with all the flanges that support the side frames set on the inside of the greenhouse. Then complete the perimeter of the gable end frame by adding the sill bar.

Next put in the vertical bars, remembering to insert the appropriate number of bolts for the horizontal and diagonal braces. Bolt the horizontal and diagonal braces to the corner brackets (the same bolt will probably hold both), fitting the bolts in the uprights through the

5 Assemble greenhouse

2. The brackets provide a fastening for the horizontal and diagonal braces and side eaves bars.

holes in the braces. Then bolt the diagonal braces to the sill bar and finally bolt both the horizontal and the diagonal braces securely to the fixed uprights.

Assemble the other end frame the same way, but add the horizontal brace in two pieces on either side of the door opening, which will be framed by the vertical bars.

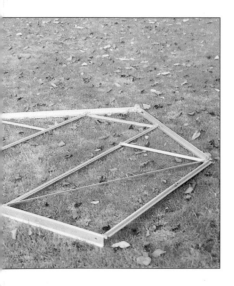

3. One gable end frame will have a split horizontal brace to allow for the door opening.

1. The end of the side eaves bar bolts to the bracket between the gable end bar and corner post.

Depending on the type of greenhouse and the maker's instructions you may have to assemble the entire framework and lift it onto the base, or assemble it directly onto the base. You will need some assistance at this stage to hold the various assemblies while the connecting bolts are put in.

Begin by bolting the two side frameworks to one of the gable end frames; the eaves bars of the former will bolt to the corner brackets between the gable end bars and corner posts. If building the greenhouse directly onto the base, position the securing screws or bolts and then bolt the second end in place. Don't fully tighten any of the bolts yet; you may even find it necessary to slacken some to allow the frames to be fitted together.

Next bolt the ridge bar between the gable end bar brackets and add the intermediate roof bars between the ridge and the eaves bars – the precise choice of position is usually left to the customer. Insert bolts in the ends of the ventilator sill, unbolt the roof bars and slide the bolt heads into their slots. Rebolt the roof bars to the eaves bar, slide the sill into position and tighten the bolts.

If the framework has been as-

2. Connect the two side frames to one gable end frame. Connect it to the base and add the other end.

sembled off the base, it should be lifted into place and secured lightly. Use a plumb line to check that the upright frame sections are truly vertical and check that the assembly is square by measuring the diagonals between the corners at sill and eaves height.

Finally, go around the framework systematically tightening all the nuts and bolts, but take care not to overtighten them in case you strip the threads.

3. If necessary temporarily disconnect one or two pieces to get the frame to fit together.

6 Add the door   7 Glazing   ▮ Options

The greenhouse door comprises a simple frame of two vertical stiles and three or four horizontal rails. Most greenhouses have sliding doors but some have hinged versions.

As with other parts of the greenhouse, begin assembly of the door frame by laying out all the parts on the ground, making sure you understood which way round they fit, and bolt or screw them together. A sliding door may have a slide bolt held to the top of one stile by the screws or bolts that hold the stile to the top rail, so it should also be added at this stage. Bolt the door wheelhousing to the top rail.

To complete the door frame, add the weatherstripping to the stiles. The vinyl molding fits into slots in the backs of the stiles and may need pinching together to allow insertion. Cut off any excess.

Bolt the sill capping piece between the feet of the upright frame members and the door track across the face of the gable end frame, adding a vertical brace to support its overhanging end. Slide the door's wheelhousing into the track, engage the bottom rail with the sill capping piece. After adjusting the wheelhousing bolts so that the weight of the door is taken evenly by the wheels, attach the door stops to the door track.

Take care when glazing the greenhouse; glass is very fragile and easily broken – always wear thick gloves when handling it. It is a good idea to make a final check for squareness of the frame before glazing, otherwise you may find that the panes won't fit.

Begin by assembling the roof ventilator which is easier to put in before glazing the rest of the frame. Slide lengths of vinyl glazing strip into the frame members and assemble the frame around the glass pane. Make sure the frame is square before fully tightening the bolts. Add the stay arm to the lower frame rail and bolt the stay pegs to the sill. Smear a little petroleum jelly along the top rail of the ventilator and slide it into the ridge bar, pushing it along until it is in position. Then position the ventilator's sill bar and tighten its bolts. Check that it moves freely and holds closed.

Then go round the rest of the greenhouse, adding glazing strips to the frame, sliding the molding along the slots in the sections.

Glaze the roof first, working from the ridge to the eaves, sliding each pane under the one above and securing them with the spring clips provided. Then glaze the sides and ends, from the bottom up, each pane overlapping the one below.

Good ventilation is essential in a greenhouse, and extra roof ventilators or louver shutters that fit between the side uprights can be added. Automatic controls for these open and close them according to temperature.

Shelving is almost a necessity and is usually available to bolt to the greenhouse frame; some versions fold away when not in use.

To protect plants from the glaring sun and reduce heat loss at night, add sliding sunshades to the roof on wire tracks.

A sliding shade provides excellent protection against a glaring sun for young plants.

1. Insert the door's wheelhousing into the track, making sure the wheels are engaged properly.

1. Handle the glass with care and wear thick gloves to protect against accidental cuts.

Roof ventilators are an easy way of improving greenhouse air flow – some open automatically.

Build a Garden Retaining Wall

A small retaining wall is no more complicated to design and construct than the average free standing garden wall, yet it could dramatically improve the appearance – and the productivity – of your garden.

Retaining walls are generally used to 'terrace' or hold a bank of earth in place, either as a structural device to stop an unstable bank from slipping away, or as an important ally to the landscape gardener in creating artificial changes of level.

If you decide that you're going to cut away an earth bank – perhaps to create a wider path or an extra driveway – you'll need a retaining wall to hold the remainder of the bank in place.

Retaining walls are fairly easy to build if you are reasonably confident about your bricklaying abilities – in practice, you will only need to use a Flemish or English bricklaying bond (see Skills Guide p. 127) and the number of times you'll have to cut a brick will be limited. Apart from the need to provide drainage holes through the wall, the only real complication will be if the wall needs to change level – you'll need to construct stepped foundations.

1 What the job involves

As with so many jobs, building a retaining wall will go smoothly if the various stages are properly thought out beforehand. Get a clear picture of what's involved with the following outline:

● excavate the site. If you are planning to cut into the existing terrain to create a terrace, this is best carried out as a two stage operation – first, landscape the ground in accordance with any plan you have for the garden; secondly, mark the line of the new bank with string and stakes, then remove soil to make room for the retaining wall.

● lay the foundations. This is one of the most important stages of the job. Although it's largely the bulk of the wall that governs its ability to hold back the soil, good foundations are needed to support its weight and stop it slipping at the bottom or settling and breaking up.

CHECKLIST

Tools
pick, shovel and spade
wheelbarrow
club hammer
wide cold chisel
trowel
level
gauge rod
concrete mixer
soft brush

Materials
bricks or blocks
coping stones (optional)
cement, sand and aggregate
gravel
vapor barrier
clay drain tiles
wooden stakes
string line

See Skills Guide pp. 127, 130–132, 134

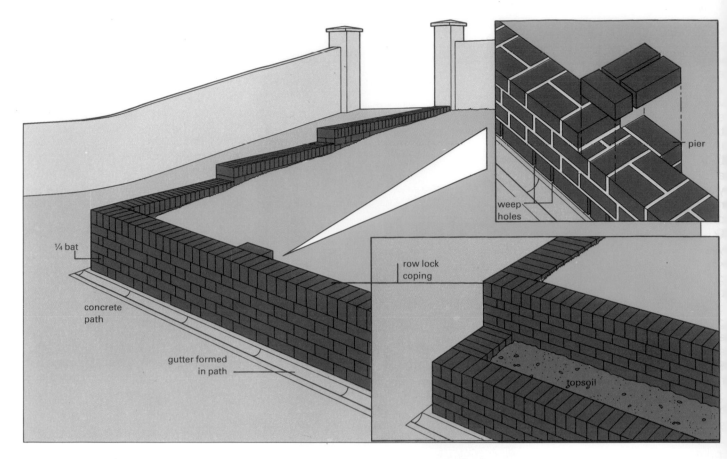

1/4 bat

concrete path

gutter formed in path

row lock coping

pier

weep holes

topsoil

Use a retaining wall to hold a garden back or to create artificial level changes or terraces

● build the wall from bricks or concrete blocks in English or Flemish bond (see Skills Guide p. 127) an '8in' thick wall will be adequate for steps of 3ft or less.
● allow for drainage. The new wall will interfere with the natural drainage of the site, so you need to make alternative arrangements for this. The normal solution to the problem is to incorporate 'weep holes' or clay drain tiles into the base of the wall, through which ground water can pass.
● top the wall with some form of coping. Retaining walls are not only attacked by the continued moisture and chemicals in the soil they retain, but also by the weather in general, just like any other garden wall. Adding a brick, stone, or concrete coping will give the wall the necessary additional protection and help create a neater finish.
● waterproof the rear face of the

wall. No matter how durable the materials from which the wall is built, the masonry (and in particular the mortar joints) are still vulnerable to erosion.

BEFORE YOU START

● if you are engaged in a complicated terracing arrangement, draw sectional diagrams of the existing bank at various points along the wall's length. These will help you confirm that the line you have chosen for the wall is feasible, and aid you in working out the quantities of materials you need (see Skills Guide p. 132).
● work out how many bricks and blocks you need — order them in advance so you can begin the construction of the wall as soon as possible after the site has been excavated.
● work out how much mortar you need to build the wall, and how much concrete is required for the foundations, then decide on the most economical and convenient

way to buy it. Even a relatively small wall can involve you in quite a lot of mortar and concrete mixing, so it may well be worth renting a concrete mixer. As with the materials you need, it is best to order this in advance so you can be sure to have it delivered and ready on the day you want to start to avoid delays.

! WATCH OUT FOR

● the weather. It's never a good idea to carry out building work during very hot or very cold spells — you'll have problems preventing concrete and mortar from either drying out too quickly, or being damaged by frost. But with a retaining wall, there is the problem of rainfall too. If the bank and the area at its foot become waterlogged, you will not only find working conditions unpleasant and difficult, but because wet soil is fairly mobile, you may find steep banks start to slip before you have had a chance to complete the wall.
● awkward soil types. Some sandy

2 Lay foundations

soils and clays are notoriously un-stable. For a small garden retaining wall this shouldn't make too much difference to what you do, but it is worth making the wall's footings wider and deeper to be on the safe side. In some parts of the country, the soil can even attack ordinary mortar and concrete. Your local building supplier should be able to advise you if this is a problem in your area, and recommend an alter-native type of concrete which will overcome it.

● underground services. Before you begin to dig make sure you know the exact position of under-ground cables and pipework. Con-tact your local utility companies to confirm the position of under-ground services. If you need to dig across a service line, they may come and do it for you.

● underestimating the strength of the wall required. Although, in most circumstances, a one brick (8in) thick wall in Flemish or English bond should be adequate to retain banks up to 3ft high, it is worth remember-ing that it is not just the bank's height that must be taken into account when assessing the wall's strength. If the slope continuing above the wall is very steep and/or very high, it will impose an additional strain. A more substantial wall incorporating buttresses and piers may therefore be necessary. In such cases, seek the advice of a structural engineer.

● instability. Excavate soil on to the 'low' side so that the 'high' side won't landslide. Provide old boards to shore up the sides of deep cut-tings. As with freestanding walls, you must build in a return or pier at each end of the wall and at intervals of no more than 10ft apart. This helps stop the wall toppling over or 'bellying out' under pressure from the soil it's holding back.

● expansion and contraction. All masonry expands and contracts as the temperature changes, and re-taining walls are no exception. With very long walls, you must make allowance for this by incorporating an expansion gap – basically an open vertical joint sealed with caulk-ing every 50ft or so.

1. Cut away the bank for access, then dig the foundation trench – aim to keep the bottom level

2. Line the bottom of the trench with gravel or rubble – compact it with a length of wood or a tamper

Earth is surprisingly heavy stuff to shift in any quantity, so take your time over the excavation. It's point-less to exhaust yourself before you start concreting the foundations.

Mark the line of the proposed bank with stakes and string, measur-ing from a fixed bench mark – say a path, fence or a manhole cover. Check that the outline is visually acceptable before you start to dig.

★ **TIP**

Save the topsoil for later. Spread a sheet of heavy duty plastic on the area in which you'd like to pile the topsoil – it'll make it easier to clean up afterwards.

Using the stakes and string as a guide, dig away the exposed subsoil to produce roughly the shape of banking or terracing you require, remembering to allow for the extra thickness of the top soil which is to be replaced. Continue excavating to leave a sufficiently wide, flat area to accommodate the wall's footings, the wall itself, and sufficient working space for yourself.

Unless the foundations are to run alongside a fixed edge, put in a second line of stakes and string parallel to the first to indicate the rear edge of the foundations.

Overlapping step foundations are needed when a wall has to change level along its length

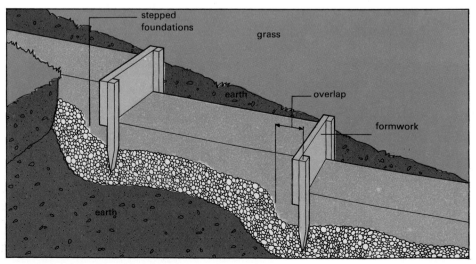

3 Build the wall

3. Pour concrete, tamp down level with the wooden formwork, then smooth off with steel float

1. Dry-lay first course, then trowel out a mortar bed. Lay bricks level with string-line

2. Build up wall, checking with gauge rod and string-line. Rake out weep holes as you go

For a typical, one-brick thick retaining wall, the concrete foundations need to be at least 6in deep, and approximately 16in wide. In clay or sandy soils, increase the size slightly.

Dig out a trench of the required size as neatly as possible, aiming for a flat bottom and straight sides so it can be used as a mold for the concrete. If the soil crumbles away, clean up the sides of the trench with some formwork, and make sure that the bottom of the trench is level as well as reasonably flat (see Skills Guide pp. 131, 134). If the wall will have to change level along its length to accommodate a slope, construct the foundations as a series of overlapping level steps, starting with the lowest and work upward.

 TIP

Don't forget to increase the width of the foundation strip at the points where you'll build piers or returns. Increase the width by roughly 6in at these points.

Line the trench with a layer of clean gravel to a depth of about 3in and ram into place. Next, pour in the concrete and work it into place. Use a 5:1 mix of aggregate and cement, but don't lay any concrete if the outside temperature is less than 37°F. Tamp down the concrete and cover with polyethylene or damp burlap and leave it to set.

With a retaining wall, the way in which the first few courses are laid can mean the difference between success and failure. It is absolutely essential that you start as you mean to continue, with a neat bonding arrangement (particularly at piers), and with level courses of brickwork rising absolutely vertically. If the wall is out of true, there is every chance that the pressure of the soil will push it over from behind.

Begin by laying out a dry run to check the bond. Follow by mixing up some mortar: in the proportion of 3 parts fine sand to 1 part masonry cement. Trowel out a layer of mortar and score a straight line down it where one edge of the wall will be. Lay the first course of bricks onto the mortar, each with one end 'buttered', and tap them down until they are level, with a ½in thick mortar bed. Build up the next courses on top of the first, making sure that the joints are a constant thickness throughout the height of the wall.

TIP

Make up a gauge rod to check that your bricklaying and mortar joints are consistent – a brick measures 2¼in in height and the mortar joints should be ½in thick, so mark off these distances on a straight strip of wood and use this rod to check the brickwork as you build it.

As you build the first few courses up, remember to provide drainage at the base of the wall. The easiest way to do this is to leave the lowest joints as open 'weep holes' every 3ft or so in the first and second courses above ground level.

Simply lay the course in the normal way, then rake out the mortar in the vertical joints that will form the 'weep holes'.

TIP

For really neat weep holes, mortar a length of ⅜in dowel into the appropriate mortar joins (angles them to slope down toward the front of the wall), then, having allowed the mortar to harden slightly, pull them out to produce neat drainage holes.

These measures are adequate if very little water will accumulate, but in more extreme cases mortar a piece of 3in clay tile in place of a half brick, every 6ft or so. The tiles will direct water through the wall from behind.

Once you've built in the drainage, keep building the wall up to the last course, finishing the pointing as you go – flush or weathered is probably the most suitable for a garden wall. Slice off the excess mortar with your trowel and finish it to the profile you want. Clean up the face of the wall with a soft brush afterwards.

4 Finish the wall

1. Add coping or row lock course. Paint brickwork, leave to dry, then brush down

Once you've built the wall to its full height, finish it off by topping it with some form of coping to neaten the top edge and help protect the wall from the weather.

The simplest way to do this is to lay a course of stretchers (bricks laid on edge with their length spanning the wall). A row lock course is not especially strong, however, so you'll need to tie in the final end bricks by bedding a strip of lead into the mortar and bending it up to hold the last stretcher in place. You'll also have to cut a brick stretcher to about two-thirds of its thickness at each end and corner of the wall.

Better still, use specially shaped brick or concrete copings – both are available in a choice of styles. Alternatively, simply cover the top of the wall with small paving slabs bedded into mortar. Whatever type of coping you decide on, make sure it has a drip groove under the edge which will overhang the wall and separate the coping from the bulk of the wall with a suitable vapor barrier – building felt, heavy polyethylene or two courses of tile – set into the mortar.

Before you go on to the next stage, you need to waterproof the rear face of the wall. A brush-on masonry sealer is simplest, but make sure it is suitable for use in this particular context. Some types may degrade after a prolonged period underground, while others won't hold back moisture that's under pressure – as it will be, having

5 Filling in

2. Protect the back of the wall with waterproofing sealer to limit moisture penetration

travelled down a slope. For a much tougher waterproofing paint on a coat of bitumen based paint or two-part epoxy resin sealant – take care not to paint above the finished soil level or the sealant will show. Alternatively, line the wall with sheets of heavy gauge polyethylene, allowing at least a 6in overlap at any joins between sheets. If you do this, position it when you add the wall's coping, so that the last mortar joint holds it in place. Trim the sheet so that it finishes a couple of courses above the wall's bottom.

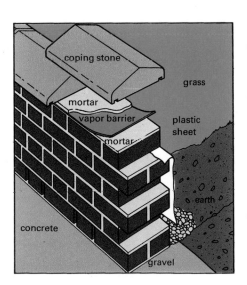

Polyethylene sheet can be used as an alternative – build into mortar course under coping

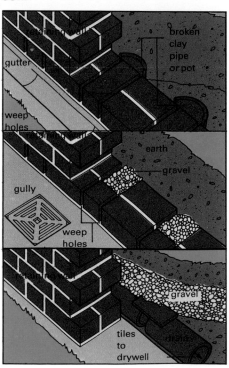

1. Backfill soil when the wall has dried thoroughly – pack down subsoil before adding topsoil

With the wall completed, backfill up to it with sub-soil. Protect the weep holes from becoming blocked by placing a piece of broken paving slab, flower pot or brick across the rear opening of each weep hole so that it lets through water but keeps the soil back. Alternatively, start backfilling around the weep holes or drain pipes with gravel rather than soil. If you have decided to use drain tiles, surround these first with gravel before you backfill so that there is a layer of gravel between wall and soil.

Garden Gate

This sturdy softwood gate is both attractive and easy to build. The flexible design enables you to modify the gate to almost any size and style.

No matter how well your home and garden is cared for, an old and ill-fitting garden gate will spoil the whole effect. A sturdy and well-fitted gate is essential, not only to the look of your home but to keep out stray animals (and keep your own pets in).

Most off-the-shelf gates are only available in a limited range of standard sizes and they are not especially durable — unless they are made from a long lasting timber such as oak, and this can cost a fortune. So if you have an awkward sized gate opening or don't like any of the off-the-shelf models, make your own gate using the plans on the following pages.

The design ensures that little vulnerable end grain is exposed to the elements as this would weaken the structure — most end grain is hidden within the two exterior faces.

A

THE GATE DESIGN

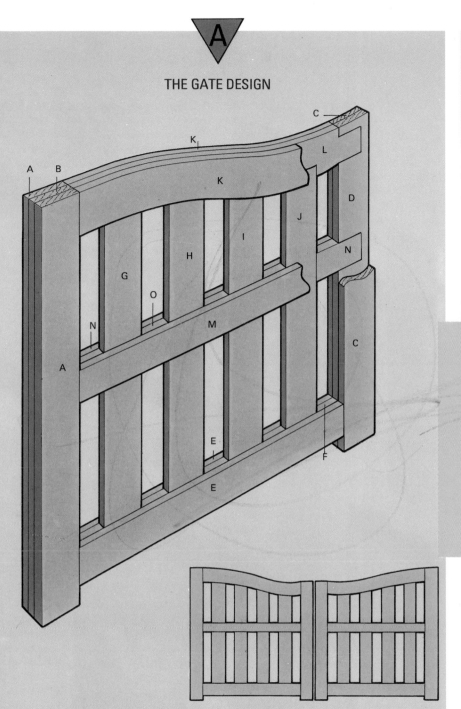

1

CUT THE COMPONENTS

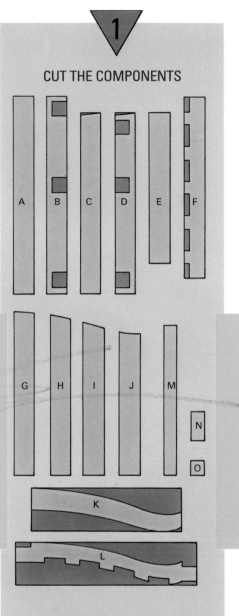

The gate is made from three layers of softwood, glued and nailed with strong, waterproof wood adhesive. This laminated construction ensures that the gate is strong and durable. 1 × 4 softwood is used for the main framework of the gate, with the cross-bar made from 1 × 3 softwood. The curved top of the gate can be drawn freehand, or with a compass on a sheet of plywood or hardboard. The sweep of the curve will dictate the size of the softwood that you can use. For a gentle curve, 1 × 6 is sufficiently deep. The size of the gate will be determined by the size of the opening between your gate posts. Allow a gap of ½in on each side of the gate for hinges and clearance. If you prefer a solid gate, omit the spacing blocks on the center panel and cut extra struts to fit in their place.

Draw the gate on a sheet of hardboard or plywood, sketching the top curve freehand or with a compass

Decide on the height and design of your gate and draw it out on plywood or hardboard, allowing ½in each side for clearance. Cut all the softwood components, except K and L.

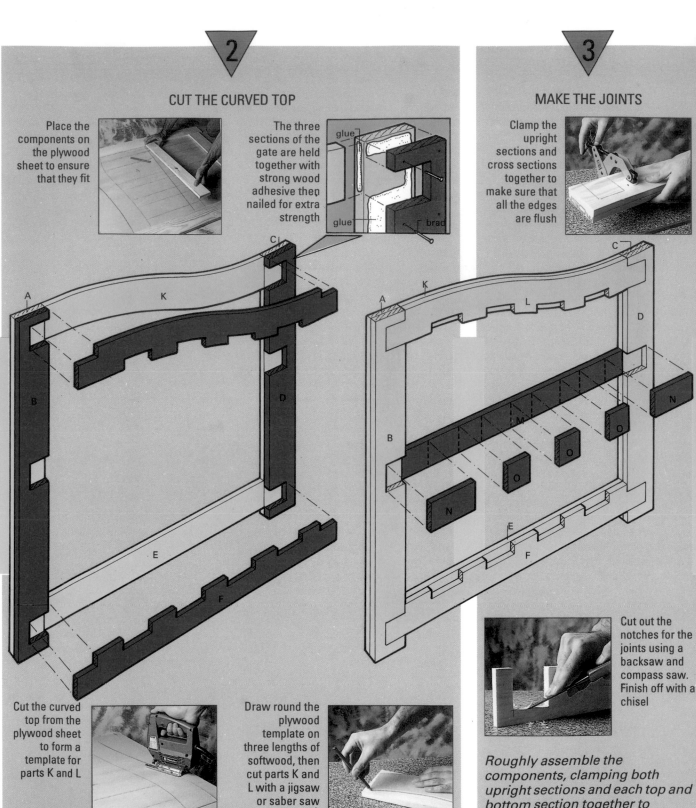

2

CUT THE CURVED TOP

Place the components on the plywood sheet to ensure that they fit

The three sections of the gate are held together with strong wood adhesive then nailed for extra strength

glue
glue
brad

Cut the curved top from the plywood sheet to form a template for parts K and L

Draw round the plywood template on three lengths of softwood, then cut parts K and L with a jigsaw or saber saw

Assemble the components loosely on the drawing to make sure that they fit. Then cut out a template for the curved top of the gate from the drawing on the plywood sheet. Draw round the

template on two lengths of softwood and cut around the line to form part K. Use a longer piece of wood for part L, drawing round the template in the same way, but adding a section to each end.

3

MAKE THE JOINTS

Clamp the upright sections and cross sections together to make sure that all the edges are flush

Cut out the notches for the joints using a backsaw and compass saw. Finish off with a chisel

Roughly assemble the components, clamping both upright sections and each top and bottom section together to ensure that each edge is flush.

If there is a slight difference in size, run a power sander over the uneven surface until it is flat.

Remove the clamps and cut the notches in parts B, D, F and L using a backsaw and a compass saw. Finish off with a chisel.

ASSEMBLE THE FRAME

Apply wood adhesive to the bottom section of the gate, then clamp the middle section in place

5

COMPLETE THE GATE

Apply adhesive to both parts N and clamp them together. Nail once the glue is dry

Glue and nail the third layer of wood onto the gate

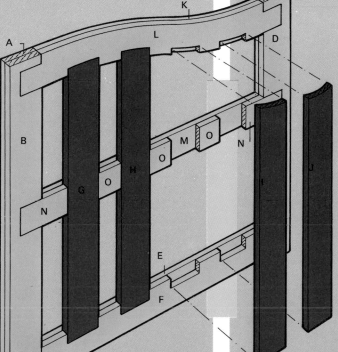

Nail the outer sections together for extra strength then position the center bar

Insert the center struts then add the spacing sections, gluing and nailing as before

Apply at least three coats of wood preservative in the color of your choice

Lay one outer framework of the gate on a flat surface and coat liberally with wood adhesive. Fit the central layer of the gate in place and clamp them together. Nail at regular intervals.

Glue and clamp parts N to both uprights and the center bar. Nail them in place once the adhesive has dried. Then glue and nail the center struts, followed by the three spacing sections,

parts O. Glue and nail the third layer, then use a power sander to round off the curved top – this encourages rain to run off, preventing water seeping through the layers of wood.

103

Adding on a Sunspace

A sunspace is the perfect bridge between house and back yard. It's somewhere to sit and enjoy the sun while there's still a nip in the spring air, and the perfect place to display and enjoy your favorite hothouse plants. It can also be a valuable home improvement in its own right. Here's how to build one from a prefabricated kit of parts.

Victorian times were the heyday of sunspace design; no respectable home of any standing was without its glass galleries and octagons in wrought iron and wood, and the emphasis was on elaborate decoration – elegant cresting to the roof ridges and gracefully arched windows. Today's sunspaces are altogether sleeker creatures, with slim glazing bars and sloping eaves among the favorite designs. However, more traditional sunrooms and even excellent copies of Victorian glass enclosures are available if these would suit the look of your property better.

Whatever type of glass enclosure you choose for your home, there's a kit of parts available for you to erect yourself. All you need to do is select the overall size of building you want, decide on the site, lay a simple base and bolt all the bits together. Add the glass, and there you have your sunspace.

Zoning regulations vary from one area to another so be sure to check to see what restrictions, if any, apply to your particular situation before you begin construction.

1 What the job involves

Choosing and erecting a prefabricated glass enclosure is an extremely simple and straightforward process – all the hard work has been done for you by the firm making the kit.

The job breaks down into a number of stages. You'll have to:
● choose the model that best suits your requirements
● work out what size you will need
● check whether zoning approval will be needed to erect it (see BEFORE YOU START)
● prepare a suitable base. This takes the form of a simple concrete slab, thicker at the edges. The enclosure can sit on this, or on a partial wall built on top
● assemble the main frame of the building and set it on its base
● secure the frame to the wall
● assemble window and door frames, and set them in place in the structure
● add the glazing panels
● seal all the joints between the base, the house wall and the glass enclosure
● secure the frame to the base when you are sure everything fits and works properly.

BEFORE YOU START

● Look carefully at the range of types and sizes available (see Options). Decide on whether you want full-height or sill-height glazing; whether the roof will be transparent or translucent; whether you prefer wood or metal (wood will need more maintenance in the future). Look at optional extras, such as opening roof sections, shelving and doors that are hinged or sliding.
● Think about how to provide direct access from the house. Is there a door or window that could be used, or will a new opening be needed?
● Think about maintenance of walls, windows, gutters etc above the enclosure. Will they be accessible?
● Check whether you will need zoning approval.

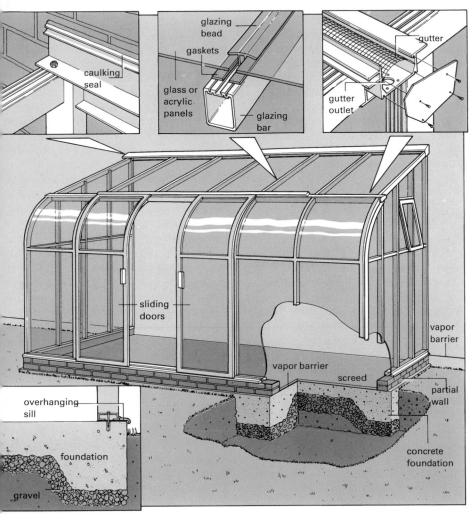

caulking seal

glazing bead

gaskets

glass or acrylic panels

glazing bar

gutter

gutter outlet

sliding doors

vapor barrier

screed

vapor barrier

partial wall

concrete foundation

overhanging sill

foundation

gravel

Glass enclosures need a firm base to stand on: they can sit either on concrete or on low brick walls

The most popular type of glass enclosure is made from bolted-up extruded aluminum

● Decide whether you will use the room as a greenhouse. If so, it's worth having a tap in it, and possibly also including a drainage hole in the floor.

● Think about safety if there are children or elderly people in the family. It may be worth having safety glazing in vulnerable areas of the building.

! WATCH OUT FOR

obstructions such as downspouts on the wall against which the enclosure will be erected. The kit manufacturer will need to know where they are so the wall junction can be modified.

● Sloping sites. It may be easier to set the enclosure on partial side walls on stepped or low-level foundations and have a suspended floor than to construct a solid base.

● Overheating in summer. You will need good through ventilation and possibly also some simple shading to stop temperatures from becoming unbearably high in hot weather. The warm air trapped inside a glass enclosure can rise in temperature very quickly and become very uncomfortable, as well as putting extra strain on your air conditioning system. However this heat absorbing ability can be very useful during the winter months.

● Snow in winter. Melting snow can slide off the house roof and crash through the enclosure unless a snowguard is set at the eaves above it.

● Burglars. Because of their thin glass and relatively flimsy construction compared with the rest of the house, glass enclosures are seldom very secure, and burglars gaining access into them will be able to attack the door into the house under cover. Make sure this door is doubly secured, or install a burglar alarm.

CHECKLIST

Tools
carpenter's square
stringline and stakes
steel tape measure
spade
bricklaying tools
assorted wrenches
level
hammer and punch
power drill
twist and masonry drill bits
screwdriver(s)

Materials
glass enclosure kit
gravel, sand and
    concrete for foundations
bricks for partial wall (optional)
acrylic sealant
screws and wallplugs
glass (unless supplied in kit)
snowguard for eaves above

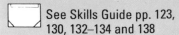

See Skills Guide pp. 123, 130, 132–134 and 138

2 Lay the base

Once you have decided on the site and size of your sunspace, the first job is to prepare a suitable base. Exactly what is required will be specified by the enclosure manufacturer, as far as both type and size are concerned, so it's important to check the instructions.

Most types are designed to stand directly on a concrete base, which may have to be a precise size to allow the base of the enclosure walls to locate over its edge. Others can be built on partial walls, which can be easier to build level on sloping sites where a solid base would require considerable excavation or back-filling.

Prepare the base in the usual way (see Skills Guide pp. 130–133), using formwork if necessary, and allow it to set completely hard before starting to erect the enclosure on it. If you won't be laying a thin coating over the base afterwards, trowel the concrete smooth while it is wet. Make sure that the base does not cross the vapor barrier in the masonry house. If a drain is to be included, build it in at this stage and add the drain run to a nearby stack or dry well. Make sure that the drainage run conforms to local building regulations. Consult the appropriate department in your area for more information about the requirements.

3 Assemble the main frame

The next stage is to assemble the main frame components of the enclosure. Precise details will vary slightly from manufacturer to manufacturer, so follow the instructions carefully throughout.

With any type, the sequence of operations starts with unpacking all the components and identifying them against the parts list.

★ **TIP**

It's a good idea to do this as soon as the kit arrives, rather than waiting until the weekend. Then you have a chance of contacting the manufacturer during working hours and obtaining any missing parts without disrupting your own plans.

With a metal-framed type, the next stage is to add all the glazing bars and door frame sections with their weather-stripping. Once this is done, the components forming the end frames of the building can be laid out in position and bolted together.

Next, prop the first end frame upright on the base in its final position (you'll need a helper for this), and attach the bottom and waist level rails to it. Prop up the other end panel and attach the other ends of the two rails. Add the ridge rail which butts up against the house wall, and the structure will stand on its own while you add any further cross rails to complete the basic skeleton of the building. Alternatively, you can assemble the skeleton then move it into position.

With the curved-eaves type, the next step is the addition of the vertical ribs that divide the building up into 'bays'. These are attached to the ridge bar at one end and to the bottom front bar at ground level, then bolted to the other horizontal rails where they intersect.

Check at this stage that the building is standing square and level. If it is not, you will have to insert shims beneath the bottom rails. Leave the connecting bolts loose at this stage to allow minor adjustments to be made to the alignment of all the components.

★ **TIP**

If the gap between the end frames and the house wall is very irregular, put up a vertical strip of wood to the wall with shims behind it and butt the frame tightly up against this. Then mark the positions of the end frames on the house wall with chalk so you can realign them if they have to be moved aside.

1. Excavate, then build up the base with gravel and concrete. Use formwork for neat edges

1. Lay out the parts and check them against each other. Bolt the main side frames together

2. Prop up the frames while you join them with front and rear members, then add uprights

4 Secure frame

With the enclosure framework complete and standing squarely on its base, you can turn your attention to securing it to the house wall. The usual way of doing this is to drive screws through the pre-drilled holes in the rear edges of each end frame and also in the ridge bar into plugs in the wall.

To drill the holes and insert the plugs, you will have to ease the end frames away from the wall slightly; that is why the chalk markings mentioned earlier are so important. Once you have drilled the holes and inserted the plugs, reposition the frame carefully and check for level and square again before driving in all the screws. Take care not to pull the frame out of square.

Add the flashing strip that will waterproof the junction between the house wall and the glass enclosure roof, ready to be dressed down over the glass as each pane is installed adjacent to the wall.

1. Mark the positions of the screws, then with a masonry bit drill holes to take plugs

2. Screw frame to wall – use a piece of wood if wall is uneven. Cover wood with lead flashing

5 Windows and doors

The next step is to assemble the door and any opening windows, ready to be attached to the frame itself.

The frames for the opening windows are put together from the short aluminum extrusions to which you attached the weatherstripping earlier; check that these are correctly positioned, then drive in the self-tapping screws to hold the frames rigid. Bolt the completed frames to the rails and ribs of the enclosure frame if they are set in the building's walls. Roof sections are usually slid into position after being located under lips in the main horizontal rails.

The door is assembled in much the same way, although special corner stiffening brackets are usually supplied to help make the door more rigid. Insert these into the mitered ends of the aluminum extrusions and then drive in self-tapping screws to lock them in place. Check that the frame is perfectly square by measuring the two diagonals; they should be equal.

★ TIP

Glaze the door before you hang it, clipping the glass into the rabbets and checking that each pane is secure. Then add the latch mechanism and put on the door handles so you can check its operation as soon as you hang it.

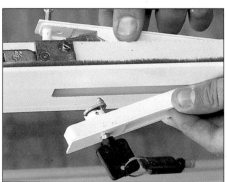

1. With doors and windows assembled, add the latches, locks, hinges and rollers

6 Add the glass

With the opening frames set in place in the enclosure's roof and walls, you can add the fixed glazing. All the panes will be supplied cut to size, and it's a simple matter to slide them into position, put in the glazing clips that secure them and add the short intermediate bars above and below each pane.

On a metal-framed type with curved eaves, all the flat panes are glass while the curved eaves sections are of acrylic sheet. Put up the flat panes first in each bar, then add the curved eaves sections. These are very flexible and can be bent easily to allow them to be sprung into the channels in the rails.

★ TIP

There is very little tolerance between the glass and the glazing bars on some models. For this reason, it helps to leave the bolts holding the rails to the ribs slightly loose so that you can ease them apart a little as you put in each pane, then tighten the bolts when each bay is complete.

Finally, add the wedge-shaped sealing strip between each pane of glass and the channels surrounding it. Press this into place around each pane as you complete a bay; then move on to the next section and repeat the process. By doing this you will not have any access problems in reaching the roof panes, since you will be able to stand on a step ladder set in the next bay of the structure.

1. Slide doors into channels one bay at a time, dress down flashings before moving on

7 Add the finishing touches

With the assembly and glazing of the sunspace complete, all that remains is to hang the door, check the operation of all the opening windows and secure the building to the base.

Start by hanging the door within its frame. With hinged doors, you may first have to add a threshold bar to the bottom rail of the main frame; this incorporates a weather-seal and may also have a stud on which the bottom corner of the door pivots. The door is then located over this bottom stud, raised to the closed position within the frame and locked in position by the addition of a top bar complete with pivot stud which is then screwed to the main frame. On some models, the door is sidehung instead using conventional hinges. With sliding systems, the door is usually top-hung from track screwed to the frame across the door opening. Whatever system is used, check that the door opens and closes smoothly and that the latch operates correctly.

Next, check that all the opening sections function correctly and that their seals are properly compressed all the way around when they are closed; if they are not, leaks may occur.

The final operation is to secure the bottom of the main frame to the base and to weatherproof the joint between the enclosure and the house wall. Drill holes through the frame, insert expanding plugs into each hole and then drive in the screws to secure it.

★ TIP

If you are making the connections close to the edge of the concrete base, drill the holes at an angle rather than vertically so that the plugs will not burst the edge of the concrete.

Run a bead of caulking all around the inside of the frame where it meets the base, and seal the joint between the end frames and the house wall in the same way if no flashing was supplied with the kit for this joint.

Complete the job by creating access into the enclosure from the house by the most suitable method, lay flooring if desired over the concrete base and move in your sun lounger and your begonias.

1. Hang the door on its hinges or rollers and adjust so that it opens smoothly. Adjust latch too

2. Clip in any remaining glazing and filler strips which are not already in place

3. Finish off the gutters and attach the downspouts – these usually clip into place

Options

There is a wide range of glass enclosures on the market nowadays, so it's a simple matter to find one that suits you and your house. They range from the traditional wood-framed sunspace with its sloping roof to ultramodern and maintenance-free buildings with slim aluminum frames and attractive curved eaves. It is possible to buy reproductions of some of the more elegant Victorian-style conservatories, although these can be surprisingly expensive. Some of these glass enclosures are not really for do-it-yourself installation and the supplying firm will prefer to erect them for you.

Remember that a sunspace can be built into an L-shaped recess too, and that it can have a solid end wall for privacy where it adjoins a neighbor's property.

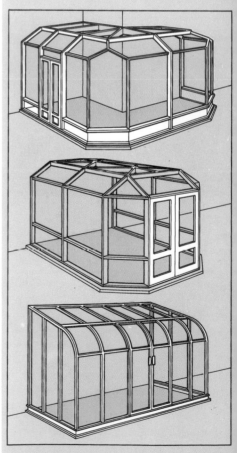

Sunspaces *come in many shapes and sizes. Custom-building will add to the cost, though*

This Skills Guide provides you with information needed to make the Outdoor Projects. If you have difficulty in finding some of the materials used in your local area, there are mail order firms which sell specialist hardware who should be able to help. Their names can be found in do-it-yourself, woodworking and cabinet-making magazines. Another source for specialist materials might be your local millwork shop or a large cabinet-making firm. Try the *Yellow Pages* too. If all else fails get advice from your local lumber yard or from an experienced woodworker for a suitable substitute.

Another point: When making projects that require carpentry, check your cutting list first, in case of differences in dimensions between your materials and those suggested here. Always take actual dimensions from the materials themselves to insure accuracy.

Using preservatives

Treating existing lumber

With the exception of naturally durable woods like teak, redwood and Western cedar, preservative treatment is essential to keep outdoor woodwork in good condition and free from decay and insect attack. There is a wide range of products available.

Creosote and other tar oil preservatives are probably the best known; they're certainly cheap and easy to apply, though they can affect sensitive skin if splashed on. Use them for fences and wooden outbuildings; keep them away from plants. They're very difficult to overpaint.

Water-borne types have toxic salts dissolved in water and can be painted over once they're dry.

Organic solvent types are similar but have a solvent base, so will penetrate wood more readily. They can be painted when dry unless they contain a silicone water-repellent additive. Some types are pigmented. All give off inflammable fumes as they dry, and the solvent smell may linger for some days after application.

Use specially formulated green preservatives near plants.

1. Preservatives are fairly runny liquids, so lay dustsheets or put down newspaper to catch drips

2. Most preservatives are best applied by brush. Start at the bottom and work upwards

3. On intricate surfaces like a trellis, use a spray gun. Mask plants, walls and so on first

4. Most preservatives are toxic to plants. Use horticultural grades in greenhouses

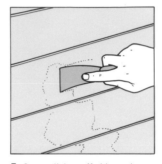

5. Scrape lichen off old wood, scrub down and apply fungicide to discourage regrowth

6. Use a pigmented preservative to enhance the appearance of garden buildings

Treating new wood

Whenever you buy wood for use outside, always buy the pre-treated type. Such wood will have been vacuum-impregnated to force preservative deep into the wood.

Even with pre-treated lumber it's a good idea to give parts that will be buried an extra treatment first. It's also essential to re-treat any saw cuts or drill holes you make as you work the lumber, since otherwise you will have created a weak link in the resistance to rot and decay.

1. Before burying posts in the ground, stand them overnight in a bucket of preservative

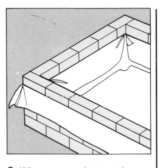

2. Where you need to treat large quantities, construct a trough with bricks and polyethylene

Preservative plugs

Where in-situ woodwork has been damaged locally by decay, it is possible to cut away and repair the rotten wood using modern resin-based fillers, and to safe-guard the existing wood next to the filled areas by drilling holes into it and inserting specially-formulated preservative plugs. These slowly release preservative into the wood, and so help to discourage the spread of any remaining fungal spores. Once the plug is in place the hole is filled ready for redecorating.

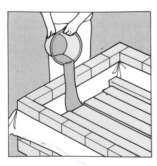

3. Pack the wood to be treated closely together in the trough and pour in the preservative

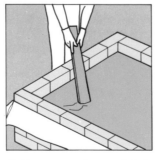

4. Many preservatives can irritate the skin. Wear rubber gloves to handle it

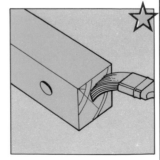

5. If you have to saw or drill treated wood, brush on more preservative for extra protection

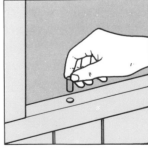

1. Drill holes into sound lumber close to the patched area, push in the plug and fill over it

Working out cutting lists

Simple carcases

Whatever you're making, you need a detailed cutting list so you can work out the most economical way of buying materials. This applies especially to man-made boards.

Start with a simple sketch (below left) containing enough detail to show how the unit is assembled – how butt joints are arranged, for example. Then write on it the overall dimensions of the unit, plus any other dimensions that depend on the unit's design such as shelf spacings and base heights. Label each component (use the same letter for identical components).

Next, measure the thickness of the board you're using. Now you can draw up simple plans (below right) and mark on them the actual dimensions of each component, taking into account the board thickness. Exaggerate this on the sketch for clarity.

Finally, write out your detailed cutting list (right), noting how many of each component to cut.

Specimen cutting list

A 13in × 20⅜in
B 13in × 30in
C 12⅜in × 28¾in (cut 2)
D 2⅜in × 12⅝in
E 20⅜in × 28¾in
F 12⅜in × 14¹⁄₁₆in (cut 2)
G 1½in × 28¾in

Rough sketch

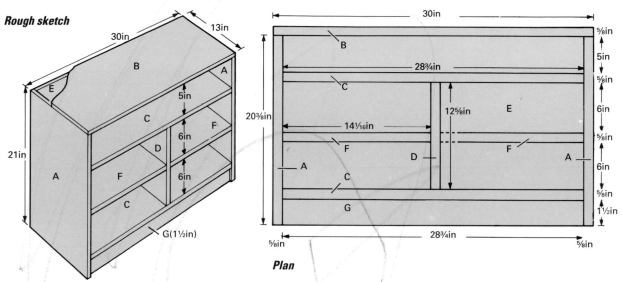

Plan

Estimating materials

Once you have a detailed cutting list, the next job is to work out the most economical way of buying your materials so as to minimize potentially expensive waste.

You must first decide on what raw material you intend to use – natural lumber, man-made board such as particle board, plywood or blockboard or a finished board such as veneered or plastic-coated particle board. Next you need to know the standard sizes in which it is available. There is a huge range of standard sizes for lumber, but man-made boards are generally available only in 8 × 4ft sheets.

Lumber is generally available in 8ft lengths, and longer, in widths varying from 2in to 12in.

With sheets, work out the most economical cutting plan on paper, by drawing the components out to scale and shuffling them round on a scale drawing of the full board until you find the best fit. Cross-check by adding up component sizes in each direction.

With lumber, simply total the lengths needed for each cross-sectional size the cutting list requires.

Specimen cutting plan

The sketches show how the components of the cutting list above can be economically cut from two standard planks of finished particleboard. Each of the components is lettered to correspond with the cutting list, and waste is shaded in color.

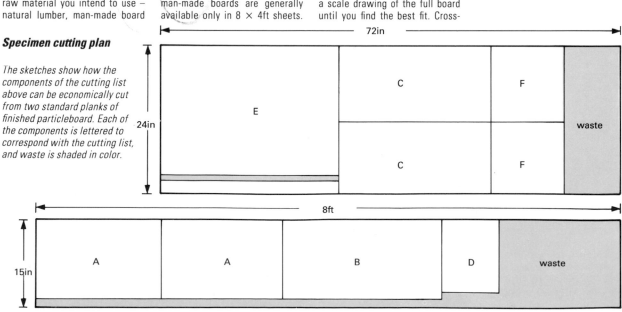

Measuring and marking wood

Marking a square end

Accurate measuring and marking is vital when cutting wood to length: errors tend to multiply and could result in ill-fitting joints and crooked construction.

Select the piece of wood you want to cut to length. Hold a try square on adjacent sides and edges to determine which are the most accurate right-angles: slide it along the board and check by looking for gaps under the blade.

Mark the truest angles with pencil symbols 'f' and 'V' (see 2) to indicate face side and face edge respectively. Always work from these marks to insure consistent marking out.

Before you cut a piece of wood to length, first insure that it has one perfectly square end from which you can take the second measurement. Hold the try square on the face side, about 2in from the end, and scribe a line across with a sharp utility knife. Turn the wood to the face edge and continue the line, then take it onto the remaining edge. Join the two edges on the final side. If the wood is square, the lines should meet.

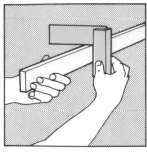

1. Use a try square to find out which two sides of the wood are perfect right angles

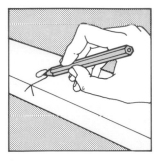

2. Mark the face side and face edge in pencil with an 'f' and a 'V' respectively

3. Square across the face side of the wood using a try square and a sharp utility knife

4. Turn the wood to the face edge and continue the score line across with the knife

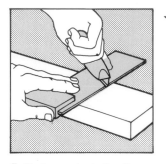

5. Flip the wood onto the other edge and scribe the line; turn it onto the final side

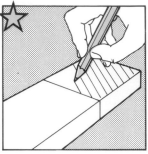

6. Cross-hatch the waste area beyond the scribed line to indicate the part to be cut off

Marking to length

Once you've established a squared end of your workpiece (see above) you can accurately mark the piece to length.

To do this you'll need a retractable steel tape measure (for long or short lengths) or a wood or plastic folding ruler for precision on shorter lengths. Measure the length you want from the squared end and draw a 'V' in pencil.

Hold a try square tight against the wood and scribe across with a sharp utility knife at the marked point.

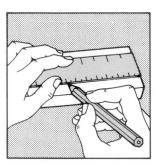

1. Measure from the squared off end with a steel or folding rule and mark the cutting line

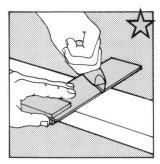

2. Square around the wood with the knife held against a try square (see above)

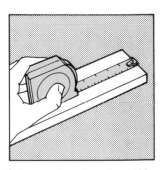

3. On a very long piece of wood it's best to use a retractable steel tape measure

Repeat marking

Mark out several pieces of wood to the same length at once.

Select face sides and edges (see above), then tape the pieces together with one set of ends aligned squarely.

Lay the wood on a flat surface then square off the taped-together ends using a try square and marking knife. Measure the length required from the outer pieces and square off with the try square from both sides. Scribe around and cut the individual pieces in the normal way.

1. To cut several pieces to the same length, tape them together and square off the ends

2. Measure and mark the length of the pieces from both sides of the bundle and square off

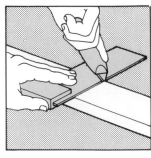

3. Release the separate pieces, then scribe around each one with a try square and knife

Cutting wood to length by hand

Using a hand saw

Wood with a larger section than a backsaw is able to cope with must be cut with a hand saw, which has no rigid spine to stop (and stiffen) the blade.

It's best to cut with the hand saw on a saw horse or clamped in the jaws of a workbench. This enables you to stand over the workpiece, even kneeling on it to steady it, and exert the correct amount of pressure as you move the saw up and down.

Take special care not to push the saw too hard, or the blade will bind and buckle under your weight – this could ruin the cut, and the saw, entirely.

Start the cut – on the waste side of the guideline – with a few backward strokes, then continue with even strokes up and down: adopt a gentle bowing action, which releases the saw teeth at each end of the cut and allows you to move smoothly into the next stroke along both cutting lines. Saw from the shoulder, using the full length of the blade, and use your finger to 'point' along the blade handle to keep the cut square.

1. *Place the wood on the saw horse or bench, kneel on it and hold the saw pointing down*

2. *Begin the cut on the waste side with a few backward strokes, lining up with your thumb*

3. *Once the saw teeth bite, start to push and pull it, keeping the blade angled down*

4. *Saw from the shoulder, not the elbow, to insure a smooth cutting action*

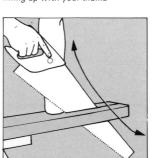

5. *Lengthen the stroke to use the whole blade and a bowing action at the ends of cut*

6. *Complete the cut with short sharp strokes so the underside of the wood won't split*

Using a backsaw

To cut lumber up to about 4in in section, you'll need a backsaw. As an aid to cutting, use a bench hook, which you can buy or make from a 10 × 9in panel of ½in plywood with a 7in long piece of 1 × 2 softwood screwed to opposite faces at each end.

To use the hook, place it on a bench or tabletop with the lower strip tight against the edge: place the wood to be cut on the base, held against the end of the top strip. To saw to a line, align the mark with the edge of the hook's strip and grip the saw with your index finger pointing along the blade to prevent it from wavering.

Draw the blade backwards two or three times over the furthest edge of the workpiece to make a notch. The blade must be on the waste side of the guideline.

Move the saw backwards and forwards rhythmically, gradually lowering the angle until it's horizontal. Cut until the teeth bite into the hook to prevent the underside of the wood splintering.

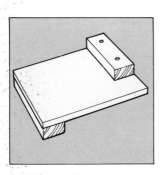

1. *Make a bench hook from a ply panel with two strips glued and screwed at each end*

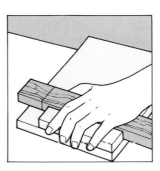

2. *Place the bench hook on the bench and grip the workpiece against the top strip*

3. *Grip the saw, index finger pointing along the blade to steady it as you cut*

4. *Draw back the saw gently a few times on the furthest edge on the waste side of the line*

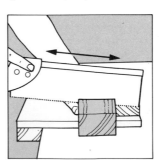

5. *Decrease the angle of the saw gradually as you move it back and forth during the cut*

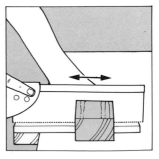

6. *Complete the cut with the blade horizontal, and cut into the bench hook fractionally*

Cutting curves

Using power tools

Even awkward curves in wood can be cut using power tools. The jigsaw or saber saw (see p. 117) is especially versatile – it can tackle softwoods up to 2¾in thick, hardwoods up to 1½in thick and most man-made boards: just guide the blade along the line but allow it to travel at its own cutting speed.

To deal with extremely complex curves in thin woods – soft or hard – a powered fret saw offers greatest controllability: you guide the workpiece itself while the saw remains stationary.

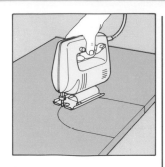

1. *Start the jigsaw then run along the marked line in one smooth, gentle motion*

2. *One jigsaw features a knob allowing the blade to turn independently for tight curves*

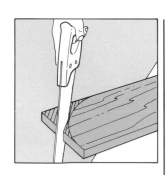

3. *A powered fret saw cuts with a vibrating blade onto which you guide the workpiece*

Curving thick wood

If you want to cut a curve in wood that's too thick to tackle with a jigsaw, you can use a combination of sawing by hand, chiselling and planing.

Mark out the curve then clamp the workpiece in a vice or workbench and make a series of saw cuts down as far as the line, using a backsaw.

Use a bevel-edged chisel and mallet to chop out the bulk of the waste. Finally, use a spokeshave to smooth the wood down to the curved line.

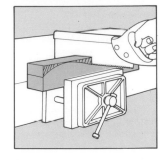

1. *Mark out the curve then make a series of backsaw cuts as far as the line*

2. *Chop out most of the waste with a chisel and mallet, cutting down into the curve*

3. *Use a spokeshave to plane away the remaining waste to create a smooth curve*

Cutting a convex edge

If you want to cut a convex edge on a piece of wood by hand, you can use a hand saw in conjunction with a planer file. Use the saw to make a straight cut across the corner to be removed, just on the waste side of the marked curve.

Make more cuts to create a series of shallow corners around the perimeter of the curve, then set the workpiece on edge in a vice and shave off the remaining waste to the marked profile to complete the curve.

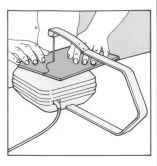

1. *Mark out the workpiece, clamp it flat and make a straight cut across the corner*

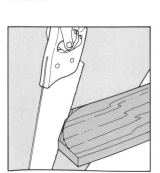

2. *Make more cuts, creating shallow corners around the length of the curve*

3. *Set the workpiece on edge and use a sharp-bladed planer file to round off the curve*

Using a coping or fret saw

To cut curves by hand in thin wood, a fine blade is needed. The coping saw has a metal frame and 6in long detachable blade with about 14 teeth per 1in which point towards the handle. For finer work a fret saw is best: its blade, 5 to 6in long, is held tensioned in a deep frame.

Blades are detachable and can be passed through a pre-drilled hole, reconnected, and used to cut internal curves within reach of the frame

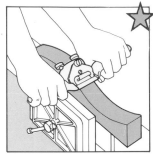

1. *If using a coping saw, support the workpiece both sides of the cutting line*

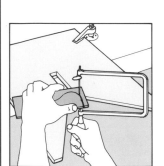

2. *With a fret saw, cuts are made vertically from below; a shaped platform allows access*

3. *For intricate curves, disconnect blade, pass through a drilled hole, then reconnect*

Shaping wood

Beveling with a plane

Cutting wood to an accurate bevel is not easy unless you have a definite guideline to follow. Set the angle precisely using a T-bevel and transfer it to both ends of the workpiece – make sure you slant it the correct way. Extend the depth along the wood with a marking gauge.

Cutting the bevel demands a steady hand and keen eye: hold the plane at the correct angle and steady it with the fingers of one hand. Plane smoothly and evenly from the shoulder.

1. *Set a T-bevel to the angle you want, then scribe a mark on each end of the timber*

2. *Set a marking gauge to the depth of the bevel and scribe along the face and edge*

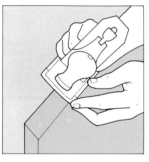

3. *Set the wood in a vise and plane along the edge at an angle until you reach the lines*

Power saw beveling

The easiest way to cut bevels is to use a power circular or saber saw. Many models have adjustable sole plates, which tilt.

Circular saws have a gauge attached to the sole plate, for setting precise angles.

Clamp the wood flat on a workbench or table with the edge to be beveled overhanging by about 3in. On long lengths, use a fence to guide the blade; if the saw has no fence, clamp a strip of wood to the workpiece parallel with the edge.

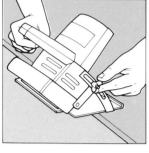

1. *Set the sole plate of a power saw to the angle required for the bevel you want*

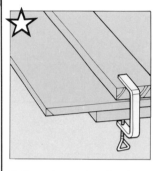

2. *Clamp the wood to a bench so that the marked out edge overhangs the edge of the bench*

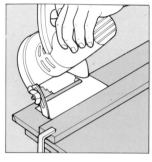

3. *Run the saw along the wood following a fence or using a strip of wood as a cutting guide*

Rounding wood in section

If you're making a chair or table leg that's to incorporate a curve the principle is basically the same as chamfering edges and rounding them over. The chamfering can be tackled using a bench plane or surform, but gentle rounding off can probably be done using sandpaper alone.

For more pronounced curves, however, the plane is required: first mark the diameter of the curve on the end of the wood then use the plane to form flat edges, successively flattening the corners until the shape becomes rounder. Sandpaper can then be used to remove the final ridges, forming a smooth curve.

It's easy to form dips in the length of the wood by planing unevenly, so make a template from a piece of card cut to the profile of the curve and run it along the workpiece at intervals to check for accuracy.

For forming a convex curve on the end of the workpiece, a surform comes in handy. For concave curves along the length, which the plane can't cope with, use a round file or surform.

1. *Mark the shape on the end of the workpiece then plane off the two adjacent corners*

2. *Continue to plane off the corners that form, creating flatter angles on the wood*

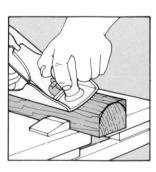

3. *Work in this way until the curve is more or less formed, then sand to remove ridges*

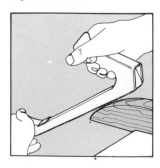

4. *A cardboard template will help you to judge whether the profile is correct*

5. *Use a surform to round off the end of the workpiece, then finish with sandpaper*

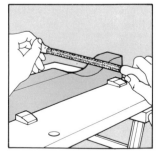

6. *Where concave curves are too tight for the plane, use a round surform to remove waste*

Drilling holes in wood (electric drill)

Setting up to drill

If you're drilling a fixed unit, you only need to insure that you drill at a right-angle: hold a try square at the side to check.

Hold a loose workpiece with C-clamps. To stop the bit from splitting the wood as it emerges at the other side (and to protect the surface you're working on) clamp the wood over scrap lumber; scraps under the clamp jaws will protect the wood.

Mark the hole position on the wood; use a bradawl to make an indent to stop the bit wandering.

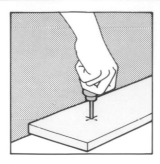

1. Mark the position of the hole with a cross, then indent the mark with a bradawl

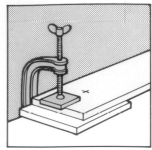

2. Clamp the workpiece over a scrap of wood, with scrap pieces under the clamp jaws

3. Hold the drill at right angles to the wood and use a try square to check the vertical

Drilling to depth

To drill to the correct depth to take a screw or dowel, use a simple guide to ensure accuracy. Chalk the bit the required distance from its tip, or wind adhesive tape around it. When this reaches the wood, you know you've drilled far enough.

A more accurate method is to use a proprietary device that can be set anywhere on the bit.

You can make your own stop from a large dowel; drill a hole through it, cut it to length and slot it onto the bit.

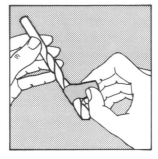

1. Wind a piece of adhesive tape around the drill bit and use the 'flag' as a depth guide

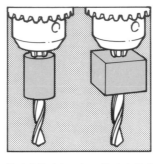

2. A drilled dowel or offcut slotted on the bit can be used as a depth guide and stop

3. A commercial depth stop and guide allows you to adjust the depth you drill to

Drilling techniques

Correct stance, grip on the drill and careful operation of the tool are necessary when drilling. Stand well-balanced and grip the handle of the drill in your right hand, the body – just behind the chuck – with your left (vice versa if you're left-handed).

Before you start to drill, punch an indent in the wood at the marked hole position using a center punch, or make a starter hole with a bradawl; this is to prevent the drill bit skidding.

Drill slowly, withdrawing the bit periodically to expel sawdust from the threads. Never force the bit: it will bind in the hole and may snap. It's worth taking stock of how in line you're drilling – keep check with a try square.

You should be able to feel when the drill bit breaks through the wood; when this happens, don't release the trigger or the bit will be held firmly in the hole. Keep it running and withdraw the bit cleanly.

On thick timber, mark out both sides accurately, drill as deep as possible then complete the hole from the other side of the wood.

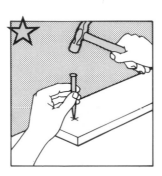

1. Make an indent on the wood with a punch or bradawl to stop the drill bit wandering

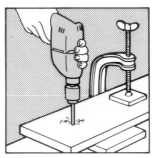

2. Drill through, periodically withdrawing to expel sawdust. Withdraw the bit with the drill running

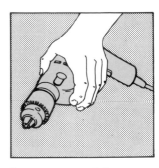

3. Some electric drills have a reverse action to make withdrawal easier and cleaner

4. You should feel the bit break through; double-check with a depth stop though

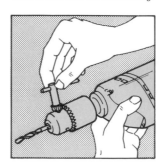

5. If the bit smokes during drilling, it needs changing, sharpening or tightening in the chuck

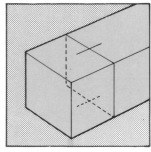

6. On thick timber it's best to drill from both sides; accurate marking and drilling is vital

Using a saber saw or jigsaw

Setting up the saber saw

The saber saw is at its best used for cornered and curved cuts in softwoods up to 2¾in thick, hardwoods up to 1½in thick and virtually any man-made boards.

Saber saw blades are straight and narrow, 3 to 4in long, and move up and down through a sole plate, cutting on the upstroke, for thin wood you need a fine blade with closely-spaced teeth; for thicker wood a coarser blade with fewer teeth at wider spacings is best.

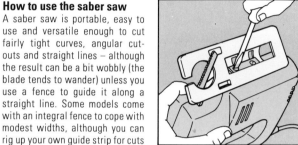

1. *Choose the correct blade to suit the material for coarse, fine or curved cuts*

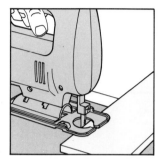

2. *Slot the blade into its socket and tighten the integral retaining screw to secure it*

3. *Set the fence to keep the same distance between the cutting line and the edge of the wood*

How to use the saber saw

A saber saw is portable, easy to use and versatile enough to cut fairly tight curves, angular cut-outs and straight lines – although the result can be a bit wobbly (the blade tends to wander) unless you use a fence to guide it along a straight line. Some models come with an integral fence to cope with modest widths, although you can rig up your own guide strip for cuts down the center of a wide sheet.

The sole plate can be angled on some saber saws.

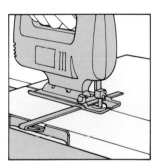

4. *On some saws the sole plate can be tilted and locked to produce a beveled cut*

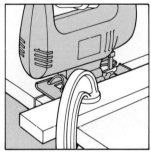

5. *With a beveling facility, it's best to make a test cut on scrap wood to check the angle*

6. *Stick tape over the cutting line on veneered/laminated surfaces to prevent splitting*

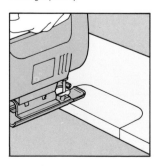

1. *Place a try square on a narrow workpiece as a visual guide to sawing squarely*

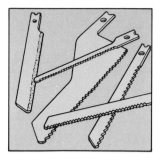

2. *Run the fence along the edge on the wood on long cuts to give a straight line*

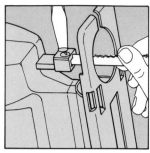

3. *For cuts in a wide sheet clamp a strip of wood to the surface and run the sole plate along it*

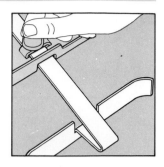

4. *Guide the saw blade along a curved cutting line in one continuous motion*

5. *To cut a notch: run blade in at each side, reverse, curve corner then remove waste*

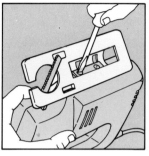

6. *For a cut-out, drill holes for the blade at the perimeter, cut between them to remove waste*

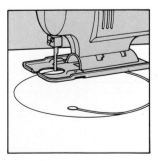

7. *To pocket-cut, rest front of sole plate on wood, switch on and ease in the blade*

8. *Set the sole plate to the required bevel or miter. Cut against a fence or wood strip*

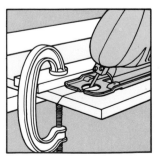

Using nails and woodscrews

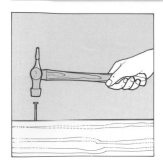

1. Hold the hammer near the end of the handle; hit the nail squarely on its head

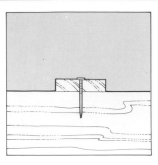

2. Nail smaller to larger, using a nail about three times as long as the workpiece

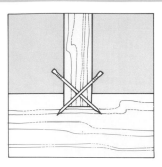

3. Toe nailing, with nails at an angle, prevents pieces being pulled apart

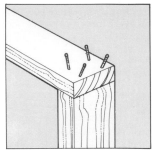

4. Dovetail nailing, for butt or dado joints, with nails driven in criss-cross fashion

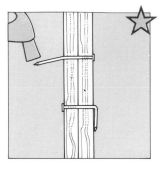

5. Clench-nailed joints are a strong choice for rough, unobtrusive carpentry work

6. Use a nail punch to sink nail heads below the surface, then conceal with filler

7. Hold and position small nails with thin card to prevent hitting your fingers

8. Lever out bent nails with a claw hammer on a wood scrap to protect the workpiece

Making guide holes

Mark the position of the screw on the strip (or whatever you're attaching). Choose the length and gauge of screw.

Wind adhesive tape around the drill bit as a guide to drilling to the correct depth, then make the clearance hole all the way through the strip.

Hold the strip in place and mark the pilot hole position through the clearance hole, using a bradawl. For gauges over No.6, drill the pilot hole. For smaller gauges use the bradawl.

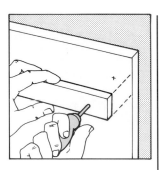

1. Drill a clearance hole to take the screw shank; mark the screw position through it

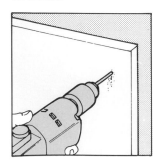

2. Drill the pilot hole to guide the screw threads and help prevent splitting of the wood

3. For very small screws, simply make a starter hole in the wood using a bradawl

Driving in the screw

Hold the item you're fastening in position and slot the screw into the clearance hole. Its tip should meet the pilot hole.

Grip the screw to support it upright (you may need to hold the fixture while you screw) and insert the screwdriver blade in the head. Turn the driver in a clockwise direction to tighten the screw. As the thread bites you can release the screw.

If the screw starts to wander at an angle, withdraw it, re-drill the pilot hole and try again.

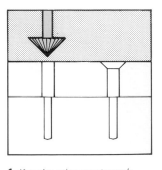

1. If you're using countersunk screws, use a hand bit to bore a recess for the head

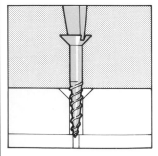

2. Insert the screw in the hole and position the screwdriver on the head; tighten clockwise

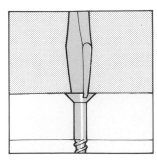

3. Don't drive in the screw too tightly: the threads may break or the workpiece may split

Clamping frames

Assembling frameworks

A frame is a structure made from thin-section wood and used extensively in the construction of chairs, tables and other furniture. A variety of joints are used to connect lengths at the corners and mid-points and these are usually glued for strength.

Glued joints need to be clamped until the adhesive has set and for frames the furniture clamp is an excellent device to use; basically a long steel spine, it has one fixed (adjustable) and one sliding jaw, so it can be altered to clamp various size frames. It's best to make two adjacent joints at a time, then clamp together, though you may be able to assemble a box shape using two or more clamps. For complete assemblies, use a web clamp.

Before glueing the joints, assemble dry to check that the components fit. Apply adhesive sparingly as too much forms a weak joint – excess will squeeze out when the clamps are tightened. Check the joint's accuracy before the adhesive hardens, then set the frame aside on a flat surface until it has set.

1. *Place the frame in the furniture clamp and locate the sliding jaw's pin in the nearest hole*

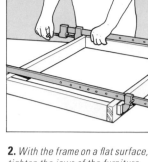

2. *With the frame on a flat surface, tighten the jaws of the furniture clamps*

3. *Use a squaring stick to check the joint; locate the nail in a corner of the frame*

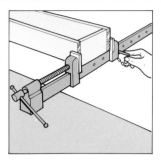

4. *Mark the opposite corner on the stick; use to check that the other diagonal is the same*

5. *Assemble one frame, then the other; always use blocks to protect the frame*

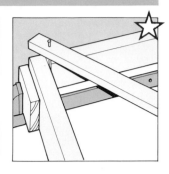

6. *With web clamps you can assemble an entire framework at one time; tighten the buckle*

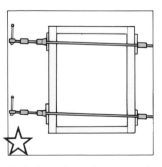

7. *An improvized clamp can be made using a length of cord and dowel, tourniquet fashion*

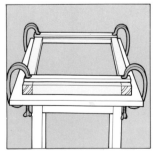

8. *Make a clamp with bolts in holes in the bench top, and wedges driven in to tighten*

Clamping picture frames

Picture frames are often delicate, thin-section molded wood which are commonly miter-jointed at the corners and secured with glue and nails.

It's essential to cut the miters accurately – using a steel miter block; a wooden one isn't accurate enough – and adequately support the butted joints while the glue sets. Clamping is also necessary to enable you to drive in the securing nails without breaking the frame. String clamps will hold the assembled frame square.

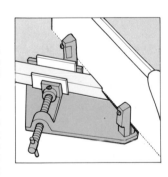

1. *Cut the molding in a steel miter block, using a sharp fine-toothed backsaw*

9. *If a frame is out of square, angle the furniture clamps to pull it back into shape*

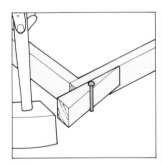

10. *A bowed frame can be clamped to a flat surface with C-clamps and strips of wood*

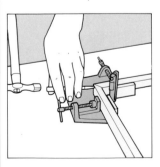

2. *Glue the miters then clamp in the miter block; drive in nails with a nail punch*

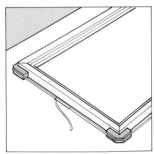

3. *A string clamp comprises corner supports and a string which can be tightened*

Making butt joints

Marking and cutting

The butt joint is the basic way to join two components; it can be used on any lumber or man-made board over ¼in thick.

The simplest joint is to butt and glue the end of one onto the face of its partner but reinforcement is usually added (see right). The marking and cutting techniques are similar for all: of prime importance is ensuring that the meeting faces are precisely square. Use a bench hook to help you grip the wood and saw straight and even.

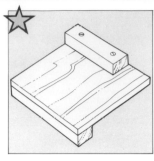

1. Make a bench hook from a plywood panel with wood strips screwed on opposite sides at each end

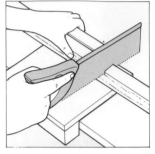

2. Hold the wood on the hook, make two backward cuts, saw angled, then decrease the angle

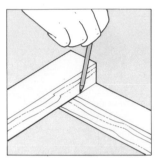

3. Bring the pieces together squarely and mark the position of each on its partner

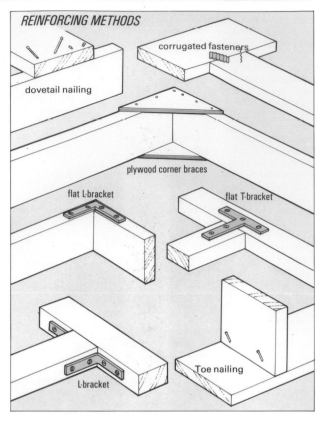

REINFORCING METHODS

corrugated fasteners

dovetail nailing

plywood corner braces

flat L-bracket

flat T-bracket

L-bracket

Toe nailing

Overlap butt joint

The overlapping butt joint is the easiest to make for T-joints, L-joints and cross joints. When reinforced with screws, it's fairly strong and neat.

Mark the components accurately with a pencil and try square (See pp. 112–113), and cut to length with a backsaw, holding the wood in a bench hook to secure it while you cut.

Piece together the components as they will be joined – support the rear end of the top piece on a scrap of wood – and mark their positions on each other, then drill the screw holes.

Use countersunk screws for strength, arranged on the wood like dice spots. For lumber up to about 2 × 3 in section, two screws are adequate; for thicker lumber five are better, so the joint won't twist.

Choose the correct size screw for the thickness of the wood and drill clearance holes through the top component to take them. Drill or bore pilot holes in the bottom piece through the clearance holes of the top one.

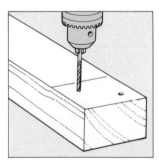

1. Clamp the top piece of wood in a vise to mark and drill the clearance holes

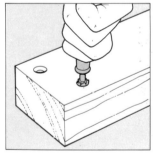

2. Use a countersinking bit to widen the mouths of the holes to recess the screw heads

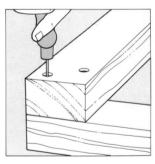

3. Assemble the pieces and bore pilot holes in the lower one with a bradawl or drill bit

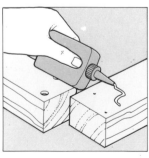

4. Smear adhesive on the meeting faces and assemble the components accurately

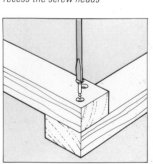

5. Drive in screws squarely, wipe off smears and set aside for the adhesive to dry

6. Reinforce a right-angled butt joint with a wood block screwed into the corner

Making dowel joints

Marking the joints

A dowel joint is a butt-joint strengthened by short lengths of cylindrical dowel glued in pre-drilled holes in the mating faces of each component.

Pre-cut hardwood dowels are sold in packs in 1/4in, 3/16in and 3/8in diameters and lengths between 1 1/4in and 1 1/2in. The dowels are fluted along their length to allow excess adhesive to escape, and are chamfered at each end to make fitting easier.

Uncut dowel lengths in a wider range of diameters are sold by lumber yards, but for simple projects pre-cut types are best.

When making a dowel joint, it's vital that the dowels are inserted perfectly squarely in the holes or the two pieces of wood won't butt up correctly.

Precise marking is essential and for this you'll need a try square, marking gauge, a pencil and either some small brads or commercial dowel pins. You'll also need some pliers for withdrawing the pins. Alternatively, buy a full dowel-joint kit which includes a jig.

1. Set a marking gauge to half the wood thickness and scribe along the end of one piece

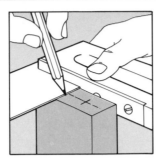

2. Divide the line into three, draw two lines at right-angles at the outer divisions

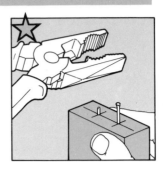

3. Tap in small brads at these points; snip off their heads so 1/8in protrudes

4. Hold the mating piece in the angle of a try square and the other piece at right-angles

5. Push the pinned end against the side of the mating piece to mark the drill holes

6. Alternatively, drill shallow holes and insert dowel pins to mark the abutting component

Drilling the dowel holes

The holes to take the dowels must be drilled perfectly squarely or the joint won't align. You can drill the holes free-hand (using a try square as a guide), but you risk the bit wandering off course, so it's easiest to use a commercial dowelling jig – the device clamps onto the workpiece as a guide.

So you don't drill too shallow or too deep a hole, make a simple depth guide by winding adhesive tape around the bit.

Use a dowel bit the same diameter as the dowel.

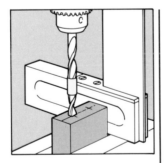

1. Drill free-hand with the wood clamped in a vise and a try square as a guide to level

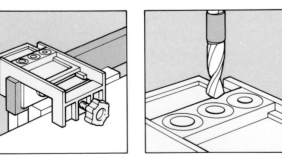

2. Clamp a dowelling jig to the wood, using scraps of wood to protect the face

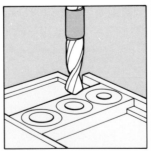

3. Insert the drill bit in the correct size hole of the jig and drill to the required depth

Inserting the dowels

Assemble the joint dry to make sure that it is accurately square before you apply glue. Check also that the holes are drilled slightly deeper than the dowel's length, in case of excess adhesive.

It's a good idea for easing the assembly of the dowel joints to slightly recess the mouths of the dowel holes, using a hand countersinking bit.

Use woodworking adhesive for glueing in the dowels, then clamp up the joint until it is completely dry.

1. Daub adhesive onto one half of the pre-cut dowel, using an old paintbrush

2. Insert the dowel in the hole and tap it in gently and squarely with a mallet

3. Apply adhesive to the protruding ends of the dowels and slot on the mating piece

Making halving joints

Corner halving joints

The corner halving joint is a simple but strong joint for all sorts of frameworks. Its strength comes from the fact that the two components interlock, providing a sizeable area for the adhesive bond. The end result is a joint that has both components flush with one another, with just a small area of end grain exposed on each side of the corner. Provided that the joint is cut neatly and accurately, the only reinforcement needed is adhesive – white woodworking adhesive for normal work, a urea formaldehyde resin adhesive for outside.

If extra reinforcement is needed, you can drive screws through the overlaps or drill through them and drive in glued dowels. Use two positioned diagonally on the overlap area.

When marking the joints, always use actual wood rather than the nominal size, and mark cutting lines with a knife rather than a pencil. Cross-hatch all waste areas in pencil and when making a series, label matching components – eg A1 and A2 – as you cut them.

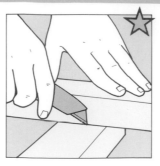

1. *First mark the width of each piece on the end of the other, using a marking knife*

2. *Check that the line is square, then continue it down onto the two sides of each piece*

3. *Set your marking gauge to half the wood thickness and scribe a line on both edges*

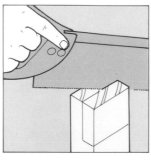

4. *Clamp each piece in a vise and saw at an angle. Finish the cut with the blade horizontal*

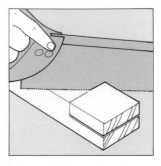

5. *Lay each piece on a bench hook and saw down the width line. Cut on the waste side*

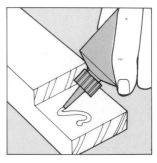

6. *Test the two parts for fit, and adjust if necessary. Then apply adhesive to one component*

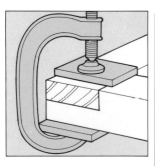

7. *Use a C-clamp and packing pieces to clamp the joint securely until the adhesive has dried*

Cross halving joints

Where the two components meet in a T or X rather than an L, a notch has to be cut in one (T) or both (X) components. As with a corner halving joint, use one component of the joint to mark the width of the cut-out on the other. Then saw down to the depth lines on the notched piece and remove the waste with a sharp chisel. Pare away a little more wood from each component if necessary to get a tight fit. Finally knock the parts apart, glue the overlap and reassemble.

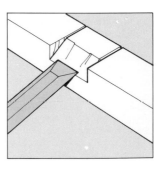

1. *When you've marked out the piece to be notched, saw down to the depth line at each side*

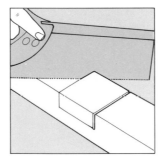

2. *Hold the wood in a vise and chisel up towards the center from the depth line at each side*

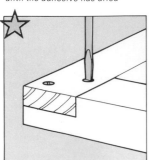

8. *If necessary, reinforce the joint with two countersunk screws or wood dowels*

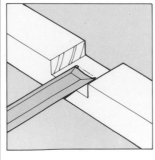

3. *Gradually flatten the 'pyramid' of waste from both sides until the cut-out has a flat base*

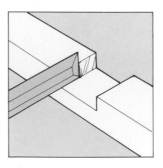

4. *Trim the sides of the notch with a sharp chisel if the two components are a tight fit*

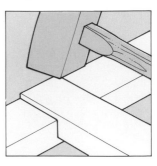

5. *Finally apply adhesive to one surface, assemble the joint with a mallet and clamp until dry*

Mixing mortar

Mortar is *cement, sand* and sometimes *lime*, mixed together with *water* to form a self-hardening 'paste'. It is generally used to bind bricks or blocks together, but may also be used to form a smooth surface coating or a shaped capping. Cement binds the sand when water is added, to make the mix strong; lime is added as a *plasticizer* to increase its workability and flexibility.

Ordinary Portland cement, the cheapest, is suitable for general purpose mixes. *White cement* is more costly and makes for decorative pointing. *Masonry cement* is pre-mixed with lime and some sand; use it for brick-laying or bedding quarry tiles.

Fine sand is used in mixes for brickwork and blockwork, bedding paving and for small repairs.

Chemical *plasticizers* are sometimes added to a mix *instead of lime* and usually come in liquid form. They are easier to mix than lime.

For small jobs, buy pre-mixed bags. For larger jobs it's cheaper to buy in bulk: cement, sand and lime are sold in bags; sand is also sold in bulk by the cubic yard.

Different strengths of mix are used for various jobs: 1 part masonry cement to 4½ parts sand is suitable for internal and external blockwork and brickwork; 1 part masonry cement to 3 parts sand is a stronger mix for mortar coatings.

One 70lb bag of masonry cement mixed with 3cu ft of sand will give enough mortar to lay about 25sq ft of brickwork.

1. *Use buckets to proportion the ingredients accurately on a smooth clean surface*

2. *Pile the measured volume of sand in a heap, crater it, then add a bucket of cement on top*

3. *Use a shovel to turn the sand and cement together repeatedly until it's a consistent color*

4. *Add plasticizer if necessary to the water – the amount will be specified – to make the mix workable*

5. *Form a crater in the center of the heap and pour in half a bucket of water gradually*

6. *Mix in the dry mortar from the sides of the crater; add more water as it is absorbed*

7. *Turn over the whole mix several times so the ingredients blend thoroughly*

Using pre-mixed mortar

Pre-packed dry mortar is sold by building centers, correctly proportioned for different purposes.

Packs range from 5lb to 70lbs which is enough to lay about 35 bricks.

Typical mixes include *sand and cement* for floor coating, laying paving and repairs; *bricklaying mortar* for general brick work and *colored mortar* for decorative pointing.

Add *white adhesive* to the water to aid adhesion and household liquid detergent as cheap plasticizer.

1. *Fill a bucket with pre-mixed mortar, then stir it to blend the ingredients thoroughly*

8. *If you've added too much water, the mix will be weakened; stiffen it with more cement*

9. *Turn the mix again, draw the shovel back in steps: ridges should be firm and smooth*

2. *Add water sparingly, mixing constantly with a length of stick or a trowel*

3. *Tip the mix onto a spotboard and turn it with the trowel to expel air and test consistency*

Using profile boards

When you're building a brick wall, it's important to lay out the foundations precisely so that the bricks can be laid square and level, otherwise you'd end up with a lopsided structure.

Profile boards are used to mark out and position the trench for the foundation slab and you can use them to indicate the position of the wall on the slab. Make two boards – one for each end of the foundation – from lengths of 1 × 2 softwood.

Drive two pegs into the ground just beyond the concrete and nail a cross-piece on top. Set it horizontal with a level. Indicate the width of the wall by driving nails into the cross-piece. Set up a profile board at the opposite end of the wall and stretch string between the nails on the top of each board.

Transfer the position of the strings to the foundation by marking a line against a level held vertically. Once you've marked where the bricks are to be laid you can remove the profile boards and strings, or build the wall up to them.

1. *Make profile boards from three lengths of wood and set at each end of the foundation*

2. *Drive nails into the top of the profile boards to indicate the width of the wall*

3. *Tie string to the nails between the profile boards as a guide to laying out the brickwork*

4. *Spread a thin bed of mortar on the foundation, under the parallel stringlines*

5. *Use a level vertically with a prop to mark the lines on the bed of mortar*

6. *Dry-lay the first two courses of bricks on the bed of mortar to check the bonding pattern*

Corners and piers

Laying out for a corner in brickwork is similar to plotting a straight run. You can set up profile boards or use bricks and stringlines to mark out the shape of the wall.

Wrap the string around the bricks and set them on the foundation. Rig up another stringline to mark the other side of the corner; set the angle at 90° using a builder's square (right).

Dry-lay the first two or three courses of bricks to check the bonding pattern: on a half-brick thick wall laid in running bond the bricks should overlap each other by half. At the corner, just butt up the end of the first brick in the return wall to the side of the last brick on the adjacent leaf. Alternate the bricks at subsequent courses.

A pier will be needed to support a straight wall at 6ft intervals: turn two bricks header-on in the first course, then lay a brick stretcher-on on the protrusion. The bond in the wall is maintained by two three-quarter bricks plus a half-brick in the second course.

1. *Use string stretched between bricks or profile boards to mark out the outline of a corner*

2. *Check the angle of the corner by holding a builder's square against the stringlines*

3. *Dry-lay the first two courses of the corner, leaving finger-thick mortar spaces between*

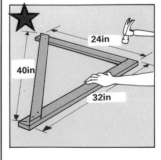

4. *Dry-lay a simple pier within the wall length by turning two bricks at right angles*

Making a builder's square

A builder's square is essential for checking that corners in brickwork are at 90°. It's used when laying out the foundation with stringlines and later during bricklaying.

You can buy metal builder's squares, but it's cheaper to make your own. Cut three pieces of 1 × 2 softwood into 24in, 32in and 40in lengths. Make a half-lap joint between the 24in and 32in lengths and add the third side.

1. *Nail together three lengths of wood in the proportions 3:4:5 to check right-angles*

The first course

The first step in bricklaying is to learn how to use the trowel: to pick up a load of mortar from the pile, cut off a slice with a sawing action, then scoop it up by sliding the trowel underneath.

To make the horizontal joints, learn how to place the mortar correctly. Hold the trowel over the site, then draw it backwards sharply, turning it over at the same time to roll the sausage off. Furrow the top of the mortar by drawing the point of the trowel back along it in ridges: this ensures suction when placing the brick, which makes for a good strong bond.

To make the vertical joints between the bricks, butter each brick with mortar before laying. Scoop up a small load of mortar on the trowel and scrape it off onto the end of the brick. Scrape the trowel down the opposite side to form a pudding shape, then furrow the top.

When you've laid and bedded the brick, slice off the excess mortar that's squeezed out and re-use it for the next joint – turn the mortar batch occasionally.

1. *Mix up some mortar then trowel enough to lay about three bricks onto the mortar bed*

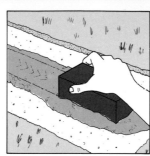

2. *Position the first brick, aligning it with the guideline on the bed of mortar*

3. *Wriggle the brick to bed it evenly then scoop off excess mortar and re-use it*

4. *Butter one end of the second brick by scraping the mortar off the trowel, forming a wedge*

5. *Furrow the wedge, then butt up the brick to the first one. Tap into place with your trowel*

6. *Lay the entire course then check the bricks' level and alignment with a level*

Following courses

Brickwork must be bonded – laid in an overlapping pattern – so that the vertical joints in one course don't align with those in the one below.

There are many bonding arrangements, some complex for a decorative effect coupled with strength. The simplest is running bond – in which the bricks are laid end-to-end and those in one course overlap those of the one above by half their length.

All joints between bricks must be consistently about ⅜in thick so the wall will rise level and square. You'll discover how much mortar to use with practice, but to help you, make a gauge rod or story pole from a 3ft length of 1 × 2 softwood marked off in brick-plus-joint increments – that's 2¾in. Hold the rod against the courses to check the joint thickness.

The other tools you'll find invaluable are a set of stakes and strings for setting each course horizontal and a level for checking vertically, horizontally and across the face of the wall.

1. *Trowel mortar onto the top of the first course of bricks and furrow it down the middle*

2. *Lay the second course of bricks, staggering the joins by half; lay cut bricks at the end*

3. *Check that the bricks aren't bowing with a level held diagonally across the faces*

4. *Use a gauge rod or story pole to check that the brick courses are rising with even joints*

5. *Slot stakes into the joint at each course; use a string as a guide to laying the course level*

6. *Build up each end of the wall, check the squareness then infill with more bricks*

A corner in running bond

When turning a corner in brick work it's necessary to maintain the bond used throughout the rest of the wall. On a half-brick thick wall in running bond (the simplest arrangement) bricks overlap each other by half and it's easy to simply turn a brick at right-angles to form the return leaf, butting its end up to the side of the last brick on the adjacent leaf. Continue the bond by alternating bricks at subsequent courses.

Lay out the first two courses of the corner dry then lay the bricks to one side of the strip foundation where they're handy for laying on mortar. Follow basic brick-laying techniques (See p. 125), ensuring that the two leaves of the wall are at right angles and that the courses rise consistently without bowing, keep checking with a level as you progress.

Build up the corners and ends of a wall first – shortening each new corner by one brick and ending in a whole brick. Fill in between the incomplete stepped arrangement making sure the stretcher is set squarely.

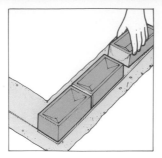

1. *Set out the foundation, scribe a mortar bed, then lay three bricks on one leg*

2. *Use a level to check that the bricks are horizontal and adjust as necessary*

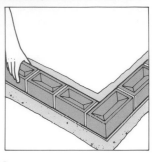

3. *Lay three bricks on the adjacent leg of the corner, end butted to side*

4. *Alternate the bond on each course. Check perpendicular with level at an angle*

5. *Rack back courses on each leg. Use a gauge rod to check courses rise consistently*

6. *Check the diagonal of the racked-back legs to insure the structure is level*

A pier in running bond

A straight wall over about 3ft high must be supported and strengthened at 6ft intervals by the inclusion of a column or pier. The pier must be tied into the bonding pattern of the wall, while allowing the front to continue uninterrupted. A pier at the end of a wall must terminate the bond neatly and squarely.

In basic running bond, an intermediate pier can be formed by turning two bricks header-on in the first course, then in the second course maintaining the bond by surrounding a half-brick (cut widthways) by two three-quarter bricks (cut widthways); the half brick should span the two header-on bricks below evenly. A single brick is laid over the protruding ends of the header-on bricks in the first course. In both cases, the cut end of the bricks should be inward facing for neatness.

A pier at the end of a running-bonded wall is formed by turning alternate bricks header-on and filling in at the courses between with half bricks to maintain the running bond.

1. *For an intermediate pier in running bond, turn two bricks header-on in course one*

2. *In course two lay a half-brick equally over the header-on bricks in course one*

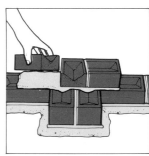

3. *Place two three-quarter bricks at each side of the half brick to keep the bond*

4. *Lay a single brick over the protruding ends of the header-on bricks to create the pier*

5. *Alternate courses one and two for the full height of the wall to tie in the pier*

6. *At the end of a wall, use a half-brick on alternate courses to make a solid pier*

English bond

Brick bonds – the pattern with which bricks are overlapped and interlocked – give strength to a wall, in addition to providing a decorative face. Of the numerous arrangements possible, English bond is the best for 8in thick walls, especially load-bearing structures.

The bond consists of one course of parallel stretchers (bricks laid lengthways), which forms the wall's thickness, alternated with a course of headers (bricks laid end-on, across the thickness of the wall). As with any brick bond, no vertical joints align, which would weaken the wall.

English bond needs either a brick cut in half lengthways (half header) in each header course or a pair of bricks cut widthways, removing one quarter of their length (¾ bats), in the stretcher courses, in order to maintain the bonding pattern.

When turning a corner in English bond, the header course on one side of the quoin (corner) becomes the stretcher course on the other side.

1. *English bond comprises alternate courses of headers and stretchers*

2. *It's worthwhile dry-laying the first few courses of bricks to test the bond*

3. *Lay the header bricks in the first course on mortar, including a half header*

4. *Start to lay the second course from the outer face of the corner with a stretcher*

5. *Complete the other half of the stretcher course laid over the header course*

6. *The third course repeats the first course; the return wall is a row of stretchers*

Flemish bond

The complex decorative design of Flemish bond – ideal for single or half-brick thick walls, is formed by alternating pairs of stretcher bricks with single bricks laid header-on. The bond is maintained at an end using a half header (a brick cut in half lengthways) and a brick laid header-on in alternate courses.

Often the headers are set slightly recessed into, or protruding from, the face of the wall which creates interesting shadow patterns. Alternatively, bricks of contrasting color and texture can be used to further heighten the decorative effect.

A right-angled corner in Flemish bond, is formed by inserting a half header and a header side by side at the corner, instead of two headers; the return wall starts with a header, then continues with alternate pairs of stretchers and single headers as normal.

In the next course of the return wall, another half header and header are used, then stretchers and headers are, once again, laid in the normal way.

1. *Flemish bond is formed by laying pairs of stretchers alternated with single headers*

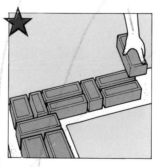

2. *Dry-lay the first few courses of the wall to make sure that the bond is correct*

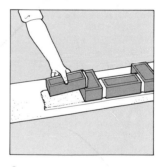

3. *Bed down the facing bricks of the first course on a bed of mortar*

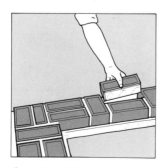

4. *Lay the bricks that form the second half of the first course between the headers*

5. *Build the second course on top of the first, stretchers over headers and vice versa*

6. *At an end (or corner) a half header and a header brick are alternated*

English garden wall bond

Garden wall bonds are variations on other standard brick bonds, but they're used for their more attractive appearance. They're also more economical, by reducing the number of headers used and introducing more stretchers without losing the essence of the bonding patterns.

English garden wall bond is a version of the strong English bond (see p. 127) and popular for boundary walls 8in thick. Although not as strong as the standard bond, it features two overlaps – one half a brick's length; the other a quarter of a brick's length – in an arrangement of three or five courses of stretchers to one of headers. A half header (brick cut in two lengthways) on the header course next to the quoin (corner) header maintains the bond. In practice, this is often replaced by two quarter-bats (¼ of a brick).

After this, the bond is repeated to the height required for the wall. With this bond, it is vital to maintain the vertical alignment of the joints on the header courses.

1. *English garden wall bond, for 8in boundary walls, saves on facing bricks*

2. *First course: leaves of headers and stretchers with a half header next to corner*

3. *Second course has headers laid over the stretchers and vice versa on return side of wall*

4. *Third course stretchers overlap the headers, and the stretchers on the return wall*

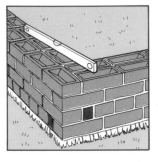

5. *Fourth course comprises stretchers again, overlapping those below by half a length*

6. *Fifth course repeats the first, sixth repeats second, and so on up the wall*

Flemish garden wall bond

Like English garden wall bond, the Flemish version is another decorative bond, economical on facing bricks, which uses three or five stretcher bricks to one header brick per course. The headers are centered in the block of stretchers in the course above, giving an attractive staggered bonding pattern to the wall.

In order to maintain the bond, a ¾-bat (brick cut widthways, with the ¼ removed) is necessary, next to each header, re-establishing the overlay at ends and corners.

Frequently used as the outer skin of a cavity wall – in its 4in thick format – the Flemish garden wall bond may include headers of a contrasting color or texture in the surrounding masonry. In some cases, headers can be recessed within or projecting from the line of the wall for interest.

When used as a half-brick skin of a cavity wall, the header bricks are cut in half widthways to make ½-bats, and the inner leaf of stretchers is omitted.

1. *Flemish garden wall bond has three or five stretchers to one header per course*

2. *Use ¾-bats next to the header brick in the first course to maintain the bond*

3. *In course two the bond is repeated, although staggered to give the correct overlap*

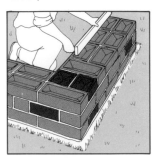

4. *The third course repeats the bonding pattern of the first course*

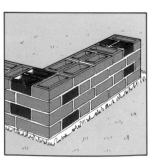

5. *Courses alternate, an end is formed by laying down extra headers*

6. *Interesting effects can be added by recessing or projecting the headers*

Building earth-retaining walls

Remodeling the ground

A sloping garden is tiring to work. However, creating a series of flat terraces will make it easier to maintain.

A retaining wall must have enough mass and adequately solid foundations to resist the lateral (sideways) pressure of the earth and the water within. For a typical wall up to 4ft high, build concrete strip foundations the length of the wall. These should be 20in wide and 6in thick, in a trench 20in below soil level.

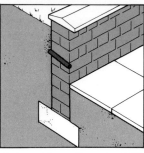

1. A retaining wall must be rigidly built on firm foundations to hold the earth

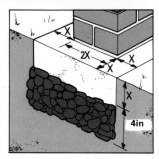

2. Decide on the size of wall, then make base extend half its width on either side and below

3. Make a series of terraces by casting stepped foundations in wooden formwork

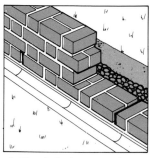

4. Weep holes (unmortared gaps between bricks) are essential to drain water from the earth

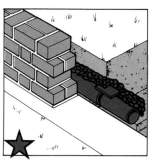

5. For waterlogged earth it's best to lay drain tiles to filter away the water

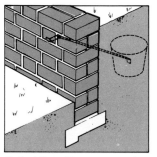

6. Stabilize with concrete castings on metal rods; a toe on the strip stops landslides

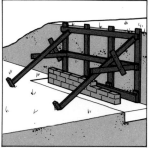

7. You may need to shore up a steep bank while the wall is built, using struts and braces

Building the wall

You can use stone, concrete blocks or bricks for the wall, but it must be bonded properly for strength (a stone wall needs to lean into the bank for this reason). Brickwork provides the strongest structure, built to a minimum thickness of 8in, or one brick thick. Use bonds such as English, Flemish or English Garden Wall (see p. 127–128).

A wall over about 4ft high should have a supporting column at each end, and at intermediate points if very long.

A retaining wall is susceptible to dampness above ground, (due to the pressure of damp earth against it) as well as under-ground. So long as there's adequate drainage in the structure, preventing the earth from becoming waterlogged, there shouldn't be too much trouble. However, it's best to incorporate a vapor barrier – heavy gauge polyethylene or coats of bituminous paint – on the back face as well.

Back-fill with a porous material such as pebbles or gravel, followed by well-compacted soil.

1. Build up the wall below ground level, using the techniques described on pp. 124–125

2. At ground level, bed short lengths of plastic pipe angled down as drainage holes

3. Continue building the wall (here in English bond) and add beveled copings at the top

4. Top the piers with capping stones bedded in mortar to stop water penetration

5. Tack heavy polyethylene to the back of the wall as a vapor barrier

6. Back-fill with granular, porous material followed by well-compacted soil

Using strings and stakes

Planning out an area of concrete on graph paper is useful when estimating materials, enables you to experiment, and is invaluable for setting alignment and levels.

Use a fixed reference point as a datum to which you can relate the various angles and gradients of the concrete slab. Strings – brightly colored nylon twine is best – and 1in sq wooden stakes are the most convenient way to set out the site when fairly level.

Tap a nail into each stake top (useful for holding the end of a tape measure) and tie the string to the first one, then stretch it to subsequent stakes and wind it around. Set the stakes about 1ft beyond the area of the slab to give you room to work; indicate the corners with more stakes. Check that corners are at 90° with a builder's square made from three pieces cf wood nailed in a triangular shape in the proportions 3:4:5 (see p. 124).

Remove the strings during site preparation and replace them to check the laying out.

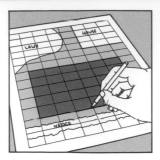

1. *Make a working drawing of the site to scale on graph paper to help with planning*

2. *Cut 1ft long stakes to size, sharpen one end and tap a nail in the top of each*

3. *Drive a stake into the ground at the site perimeter, using a common reference point*

4. *Sink a second stake the required distance from the first, along the same side*

5. *Tie string to two more stakes, stretch over the first two and drive into the ground*

6. *Set strings and stakes for the sides of the proposed slab at right-angles to the first*

7. *Hold a builder's square at the corners to check that they're at right-angles*

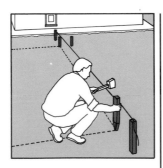

8. *Sink the remaining two corner stakes the correct distance from the first ones*

Laying out an irregular site

An odd-shaped area of concrete is more complicated to lay out, especially if it has curves – a path winding down the yard, for instance. Start with a sketch on graph paper, then transfer this to the site, using a stringline for the longest edge and one at right-angles for the shortest.

Measure along the stringlines and at right-angles to them in increments relative to your scale plan to give you the positions for the marker stakes.

1. *Set up right-angle strings for the longest and shortest sides of a long, curving site*

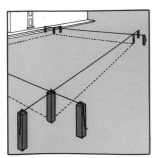

9. *Stretch the fourth string between two more stakes sunk outside the slab perimeter*

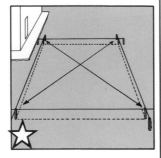

10. *Measure the diagonals between corners: if they're equal, the site is square*

2. *Measure along the longest string in increments proportionate to your plan*

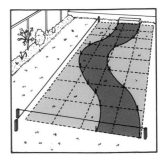

3. *Measure along the shortest string: plot lines at 90° and where they cross sink a stake*

Using formwork

Setting up formwork

Formwork is a wood frame used to mold and retain a wet concrete mix until it has set. It's also used as a guide to leveling the concrete to the correct thickness, by drawing a strike board across the top edge.

Boards for formwork must be reasonably straight-edged and free from serious warps, in thicknesses from ½ to ¾in, dependent on the area of the slab of concrete. Old floorboards are ideal for formwork.

The site must be basically level-led and laid out with strings and stakes (see p. 130) before the formwork can be set. Position the boards on edge along your guide-lines and nail them to sturdy stakes driven into the ground just outside the site. There's no need to cut the boards precisely to length: butt the end of one to the face of another at corners and secure to a stake. On long slabs – a path, for instance – butt board ends to end and nail to two stakes.

Set the boards level (or with a drainage fall) so the stakes don't protrude above the top.

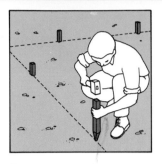

1. *Drive pointed stakes into the ground outside the site at 4ft intervals*

2. *Set the stakes to the correct depth with a level and straight-edged plank*

3. *Nail the boards to the stakes, butted end-to-face at corners and leveled*

4. *Check that the formwork is at right angles at the corners using a builder's square*

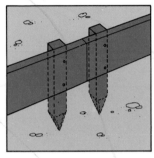

5. *On a long run, butt boards end-to-end and secure by nailing to two stakes*

6. *Form curves by making saw cuts across the boards at intervals and nail to stakes*

Formwork for large castings

Formwork of this type is used to mold and retain bulky concrete castings – a flight of steps or retaining wall.

You can use softwood boards, but for deep castings ¾ or 1in thick plywood is often better, especially for the sides of the 'box'. Set stakes and braces to support the panels, especially at the joints – the weak points.

Coat the inner faces of the boards with old engine oil to prevent the concrete sticking.

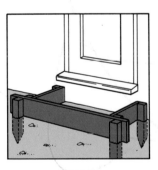

1. *Arrange formwork for a single step with boards, stakes and corner cleats*

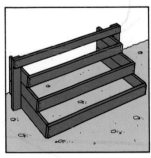

2. *Assemble formwork for a flight of steps with stacked trays braced and staked*

An earth-retaining wall

An earth-retaining wall can be cast in concrete within heavy formwork of 1in thick boards or plywood on suitable foundations. Reinforcement (iron rods or metal mesh) is necessary for the wall itself, and sturdy supports of at least 2 × 4 section, driven about 12in into the ground, and similarly braced, are vital to keep the formwork upright.

Dividing braces are also neces-sary to space out the walls of the formwork.

3. *Support the risers with an angled brace and stakes rather than nailing the pieces*

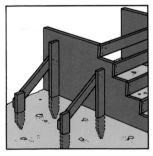

4. *For deep castings, use plywood side panels with diagonal braces and stakes*

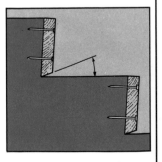

5. *Bevel the underside of the risers to enable the trowel to reach into the angle*

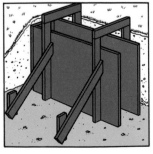

1. *Set up the sides of the formwork, then brace the vertical supports at the top*

Laying out flat surfaces

When you're casting concrete it's important to get the surface flat: allow for this during the stage of site preparation.

Lay out the area (see p. 130), using strings and stakes, taken from a prime datum stake or bench-mark driven into the ground to a depth that corresponds with the finished level of the slab. If the slab is to be built against a masonry wall, set the top of the datum stake below the vapor barrier to prevent water splashing up above it from the slab – 6in below is the recommended distance.

Rest one end of a long straight-edged plank on the datum stake and the other end on the closest stake marking the perimeter of the proposed slab. Lay a level on top of the plank – when the bubble is central, the stakes are set horizontal. Adjust the level by raising or lowering the second stake (not the first one, which you know to be correct). Other stakes driven into the ground over the remaining area of the slab can be leveled to match the already leveled stakes.

1. *Place a plank and level on the prime datum and adjacent stake to check levels*

2. *Tap down or raise the second stake until the bubble in the level registers horizontal*

3. *Move on from the second stake to the subsequent perimeter stakes, leveling as before*

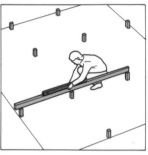

4. *Level the area of the site by driving in and leveling intermediate stakes*

5. *Set up your formwork around the proposed slab and check along it with the level*

6. *Don't forget to check across the formwork to insure the sides are level*

Laying out gradients

No large concrete slab laid outside should be totally horizontal or rainwater will tend to collect on the surface. It's necessary to set such a slab on a slight cant to enable the surplus water to drain away freely. On a sloping site, ensure that the slope is even, on a flat site, set one side about 1in lower than the other, using a scrap of wood called a 'shim' under the level on the lower side of the slab to check the gradient.

The surface of the slab should still be flat enough so that you can build on it or use it as a hard surface for patio, path or drive-way. Working from a prime datum stake aligned with a given reference point (see above), aim to set first the ground-modeling stakes, then the concrete's formwork mold to a consistent crossfall so that rainwater will run to a drainage point – a dry well or gully.

If the slab is to be built against a house or outbuilding, ensure that the crossfall is away from the walls, even if the ground slopes towards the building.

1. *On a flat site, set the drainage crossfall away from the walls to a drainage point*

2. *Place a shim under the plank and level on what will be the lower side of the slab*

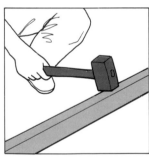

3. *With the higher side set to the prime datum or bench mark adjust the height of the lower formwork*

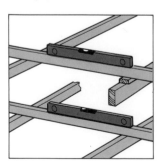

4. *When the level bubble registers centrally, the fall is set accurately*

5. *If the ground slopes towards a building, take the slab below floor level*

6. *Divert the surface water by gutter to a drain or dry well at one side of the slab*

Laying a concrete slab

Casting the mix

The depth of concrete you need to cast depends on how firm the ground is and what the slab is to be used for: for a base for a garden shed, 3in is suitable; for a driveway, 4in is adequate. On soft clay or poor subsoils, increase these thicknesses by 1–2in.

Once you know how thick the slab is to be, you'll be able to excavate the foundations accordingly, add the correct depth of gravel base and calculate how much concrete you'll need by working out the volume of the site.

For a general purpose concrete mix for a slab 3in thick and over, use the proportions of 1 bucket of cement: 2½ buckets sand: 4 buckets coarse aggregate. If the slab is to be laid on sloping ground, the mix should be stiff to prevent slumping and the area divided into a series of bays.

Cast the concrete direct on the gravel base and compact it level with the formwork mold to dispel air bubbles, which would weaken it.

1. *Wheel loads of concrete to the site on a plank path and tip them onto the gravel*

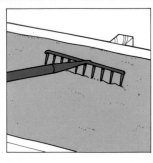

2. *Rake the wet concrete level so it's slightly above the tops of the formwork*

3. *Slice a shovel into the mix at the sides and work the concrete well into place*

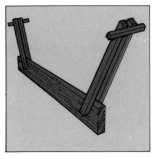

4. *Make a strike board from heavy lumber. It'll be easier to use if you add handles*

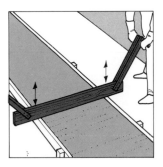

5. *Place the beam across the slab and compact it using a chopping motion*

6. *Work along the slab with a sawing action to level the concrete with the formwork*

7. *Fill any hollows left by the strike board with concrete, then repeat the process*

8. *When you've tamped the concrete thoroughly, tap the formwork to settle the mix*

Finishing and curing

Leave the slab with the rough texture left by the strike board or apply a smooth surface with a steel or wooden trowel; for a non-slip finish, run a stiff-bristled broom across.

The slab must 'cure' so that it sets, without drying out too quickly, which could cause cracking. Cover with heavy gauge polyethylene held down with bricks. You shouldn't lay concrete during frosty weather but if a cold snap strikes, insulate the mix with sand over the sheet.

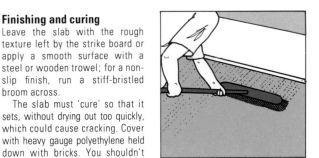

1. *Use a bristle brush to form a regular, non-slip finish or polish with a trowel*

9. *On a large slab, set in thin softwood strips at 10ft intervals as expansion joints*

10. *If you're laying the slab up against a wall, cast and compact the mix in bays*

2. *Cover the slab with heavy gauge polyethylene and leave to cure for about four days*

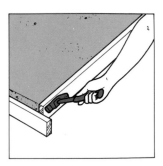

3. *You can remove the formwork after only 24 hours but it's best to leave until cured*

Laying strip foundations

Digging the trench

Strip foundations set in a trench are used as footings for garden walls or small structures. They should be twice the width of the masonry, half as deep as they are wide and should project beyond the ends by half the width of the masonry. For a wall over six courses high, a trench about 16in deep is needed.

To mark out the trench, hammer pairs of 2ft long 1 × 2 stakes into the ground at each end and nail cross-pieces on top. Drive nails into each cross-piece the width of the trench apart and tie string between. Sprinkle sand over the strings to transfer their positions to the ground.

Dig the trench to depth, then set stakes at 2ft intervals along its length so they protrude by the depth of concrete. Place a plank and level on the stakes to check their level. On soft ground add gravel and ram down. Shovel in the concrete and tamp to dispel air bubbles so it's level with the stakes. Cover with polyethylene and leave to harden for 24 hours before building on it.

1. Set up profile boards at each end of the proposed trench and outside the foundation line

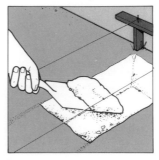

2. Measure the width of the trench on the cross-pieces and drive in nails at these points

3. Tie string lines between the nails to indicate the width and length of the trench

4. Sprinkle sand along the stringline to transfer their positions to the ground

5. Dig the trench to the depth required, checking that it's consistently deep

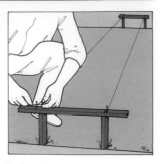

6. Drive stakes into the base of the trench so they protrude by the depth of concrete needed

7. Span the stakes with a plank and level and adjust them so they're horizontal

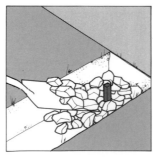

8. Shovel in gravel if the soil is soft, then ram this down with a sledgehammer

9. Tip the concrete mix into the trench and work it in order to dispel air bubbles

10. Use a length of heavy board to compact the concrete to the level of the stake tops

11. Place a level on top of a plank to check that the strip is absolutely horizontal

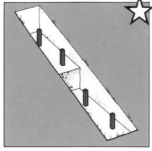

12. On sloping or uneven ground step the foundation trench to accommodate changing levels

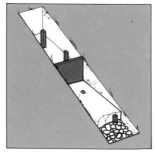

13. Fill the lower step then use a board to retain the concrete for the top step

14. For a right-angled wall, set up two pairs of profile boards and stringlines

Building freestanding steps

How the steps are built

Steps are vital to provide access in a split level garden, and a free-standing flight is the best choice to rise from ground level to a higher, terraced level – a raised lawn, driveway or patio, for instance.

The risers are built from bricks or blocks on cast concrete strip foundations (or a slab foundation if more than about three steps high). Risers comprise U-shaped retaining walls two courses high, back filled with rubble and topped with standard concrete slab treads.

Step dimensions

The scale of the flight is important for safe, comfortable use and should be neither too steep (and so tiring to climb) nor too shallow (and a trip hazard). Steps must be the same height and depth throughout, with an overlapping 'nosing' to accentuate the front edges. The overall riser should be between 4 and 7½in and the treads at least 11½in from front to back, so there's enough room to take the foot when descending.

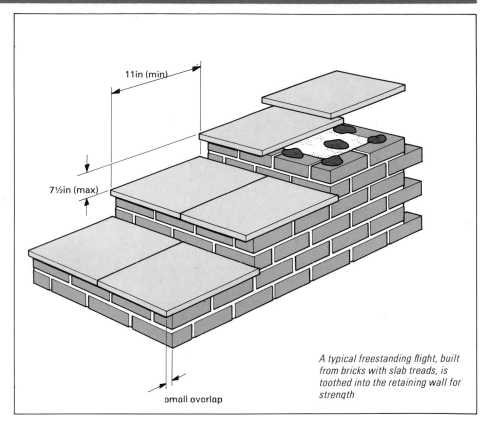

11in (min)

7½in (max)

small overlap

A typical freestanding flight, built from bricks with slab treads, is toothed into the retaining wall for strength

1. *Cast strip foundations for the risers; set up stringlines as a guide to bricklaying*

2. *Lay two courses of bricks for the first riser on foundations using a running bond*

3. *Bond riser to back wall by toothing alternate bricks into chopped-out holes*

4. *Leave the mortar to stiffen then shovel rubble behind the riser and compact thoroughly*

5. *Spread a binding layer of coarse sand over the rubble to fill voids and scrape level*

6. *Build subsequent risers over the first, staggering joins and checking courses are consistent*

7. *Lay slab treads on the risers bedded on five dabs of mortar, overhanging by about 1 in*

8. *Set the slab treads to slope forward slightly for drainage by packing at the back with mortar*

Planning the steps

Garden steps can be built into an existing bank, using the ground as foundations. Bricks, walling blocks or natural stone are best for the risers, and slabs for the treads. You can use bricks, blocks (even quarry tiles) for the treads, too, but aim to complement other materials used in the garden.

Steps should conform to basic dimensions (constant throughout the flight) for comfortable and safe walking: risers 4–7½in high (two brick or block courses); treads no less than 11½in from front to back – 24in wide for one, 5ft wide for two or more. A tread nosing (defining the step in shadow) should project beyond the riser no less than 1in, treads should slope forward slightly for drainage. A flight shouldn't have more than ten steps without a landing.

To determine the number of steps you'll need, measure the vertical height of the slope then divide the height of a riser (plus tread thickness) into this figure to give the number of risers.

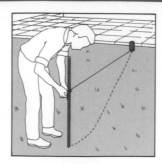

1. Set a string level between a stake (top) and cane (base) to give the height of the slope

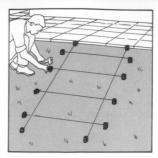

2. Set strings between stakes to define the sides of the flight and the tread nosings

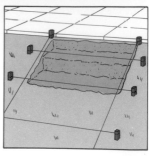

3. Starting at the top of the bank, dig out the rough shape of the steps with a spade

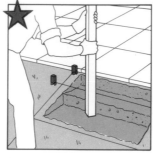

4. Compact the earth within the strings using a heavy wooden post or a sledgehammer

5. Work down to the base of the bank, excavating the rough shape of the flight

6. Dig below and behind the nosing strings allowing for slab treads and block risers

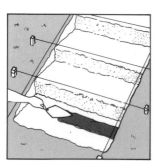

7. Cast a concrete footing at the base then trowel on mortar for the first riser

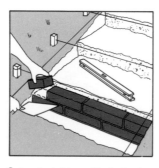

8. Lay the bricks on blocks for the first riser and check that they're level and square

9. Back-fill behind the riser using gravel and compact it level with the top

10. Add coarse gravel to the first tread position then tamp this down thoroughly

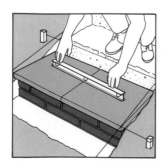

11. Bed the treads on mortar with a slight fall to front. Align nosings with the string

12. Lay the second riser on the back of the first tread or behind it on coarse gravel

13. Back-fill with gravel then lay the second tread and subsequent steps

14. Point the joints on the risers then brush a dry mortar mix into gaps between slabs

Setting posts in concrete

Wood and steel posts

There are several jobs that are likely to involve setting up a post upright in a firm base – erecting fence posts, building garden structures like pergolas, putting up a carport, even installing a rotary clothes line. In all these cases the end result must be a post (or posts) set truly vertical and solidly supported.

The first stage is to dig out a hole of the right depth. For fence posts up to about 4ft high, dig a 18in deep hole; for taller posts dig down 2ft. Then excavate the hole by a further 6in to allow for a base of coarse gravel on which the foot of the post will stand. This improves drainage and helps to discourage decay.

Always use preservative-treated wood, and give the part of the post that will be buried a further treatment by leaving it to stand overnight in a bucket of preservative. If you're using galvanized steel posts, treat the buried end with at least two coats of bituminous paint to help prevent corrosion eating into it below ground level.

1. *Dig a hole of the correct depth and roughly a spade's width; try to keep the sides vertical*

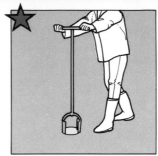

2. *Alternatively, use a post hole borer, which removes a core of soil easily and neatly*

3. *Put some coarse gravel in the hole and tamp down securely*

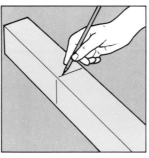

4. *Mark the required above-ground height clearly on the post as a guide to positioning it*

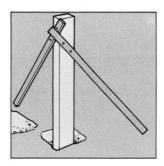

5. *Set the post in the hole, check that the mark is at ground level and add two wooden braces*

6. *Check that the post is vertical by holding a level against one face, then the other*

7. *Carefully pack in some more gravel round the post to within 6in of ground level*

8. *Shovel in concrete round the post to just above ground level, and tamp it down well*

Rotary clothes line

Rotary (and some fixed) clothes lines are designed to stand in a tubular socket set flush with the ground level. It's obviously essential that the socket holds the post upright, and that it is secure enough to withstand wind pressure on a line full of washing.

Setting the socket in concrete is the best answer. It can be sited in the lawn or, perhaps better for winter use, in the center of a paved area. In the latter case, make sure there is room for the washing to blow freely.

1. *Set the socket on a gravel base so its top is at ground level, then pack concrete round it*

9. *Trowel off the surface of the concrete to a slope that will throw water away from the post*

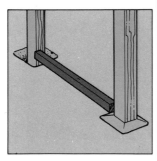

10. *If you're setting a line of fence posts, use a spacer board to set the distance between them*

2. *Slot a pole in the socket and add two braces so you can check that the socket is vertical*

3. *Add more concrete and trowel it smooth. Use a flowerpot for a mold if the socket is set in a lawn*

137

Using caulking and mastics

Where mastic is used

Mastics are flexible fillers which don't set hard, but which form a skin that can be painted. They're ideal for filling gaps or cracks where there's likely to be some movement in the surrounding surfaces, or due to natural expansion or contraction of the materials used. A selection of uses are illustrated below.

Various types of mastics are made to suit different situations: oil-based mastic resists moisture and inclement weather; silicone or acrylic sealants likewise bar moisture and remain flexible over a much wider temperature range and are thus useful for bathrooms; bituminous mastic, usually black and reinforced with rubber, is best for sealing gutter joints and cracks in flashings and roofing felt (a special primer is required).

Preparing mastic for use

Mastics come in various forms and types of container – in strips, toothpaste-like tubes, rigid tubes with plunger, cartridges with finger-pressure triggers and those which require a special gun.

Whatever the type, the mastic is applied in much the same way: a bead of sealant is simply squeezed into the gap. Gaps wider than about ⅛in may require filling with rope to prevent the mastic sinking into and below the gap.

Tube containers may simply require piercing to release the mastic. Other containers have pointed nozzles, the end of which you cut off at an angle to produce the thickness of bead required to fill the gap. It's best to start with a small bead.

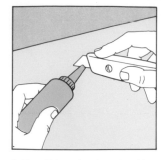

1. *Cut off the pointed nozzle with a utility knife to give the bead thickness required*

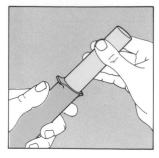

2. *Insert the plunger in the end of a cartridge container to force out the mastic*

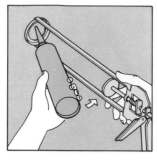

3. *Alternatively, slip the mastic cartridge into the spring-loaded gun and align the plunger*

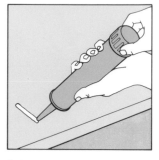

4. *Squeeze out some mastic on a practice area to achieve the size of bead required*

5. *On a cold day, soak the mastic container in a bucket of warm water to soften it*

1. *Run a bead of caulking down the gap between a window or door frame and the masonry*

2. *Fill a hole in a wall where a pipe has been removed using a weatherproof sealant*

3. *Seal minor cracks in walls with an oil-based mastic; then paint over after a few days*

4. *Cracks in roofing felt can be sealed with a rubber-reinforced bituminous mastic*

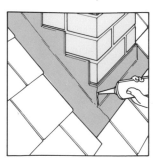

5. *Seal a torn or punctured flashing where a roof meets a wall or at a chimney*

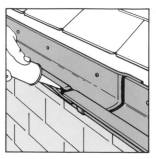

6. *Leaky metal gutter joints can be sealed with a bitumen mastic, primed then painted*

7. *Prevent moisture seeping behind an outside wall light with a bead of caulking*

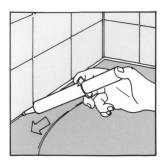

8. *Run a bead of silicone or acrylic sealant along gaps around bath and sink*

Repairing fascias and soffits

Protecting the eaves

Fascias and soffits are attached to the protruding ends of rafters and joists to protect them from the elements. Fascias also provide a fastening place for the gutters and soffits line the undersides of the joists where they project beyond the wall line.

Because of their inaccessible location and because they are more susceptible to deterioration than many other parts of the house, soffits and fascias often escape maintenance until the damage is done.

You can make a preliminary examination from ground level, but if you suspect deterioration you must take a closer look.

Replacement of fascias and soffits is straightforward: they are nailed to the roof members or to blocks attached to the joists. The soffit may be rabbeted to fit into a groove on the back of the fascia, but this is not vital.

If only a section of fascia or soffit is damaged you may be able to cut it back to the nearest joist or rafter and join in a new piece of wood.

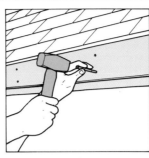

1. Release the gutter attachment from a rotten fascia, free the sections and lower to ground

2. Extract the nails holding the fascia or punch them all the way through if stubborn

3. Pull fascia away (you may need a crowbar), but take care not to damage the roofing

4. Treat the replacement thoroughly with preservative before nailing in position

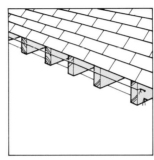

5. Tie strings along ends and underside the roof members as a check for misalignment

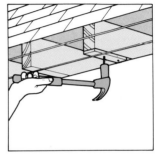

6. Nail wooden packing to gaps or saw off excess where strings are forced out of line

7. Hold up soffit; mark a line indicating the center of the nearest joist to its end

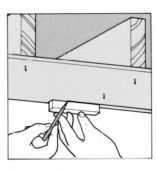

8. Nail soffit in place and scribe wall profile along it with pencil and wood block

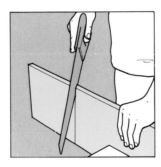

9. Remove the soffit and cut it to length, mitering the ends for a watertight join

10. Saw along the scribed line or use a surform if the waste is minimal

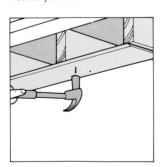

11. Re-nail the soffit to the undersides of the joists; miter up, using galvanized nails

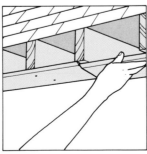

12. Set the next section of soffit, butting the mitered end tightly to the first, then nail

13. Cut the fascia board to length, then lift it up to the roof and set level

14. Nail the fascia board in place through the face into rafters or joists

▲ INDEX